Markets of the Seventies

Markets of the Seventies

The Unwinding U.S. Economy

By the Editors of FORTUNE

The Viking Press · New York

Contents

Introduction

THIS BOOK IS ABOUT THE FUTURE—more particularly, the future of the United States economy, especially various important segments of it, into the 1970s. Composed of a series on "The U.S. Economy in a New Era" that appeared in *Fortune* during 1967, the book is published in the expectation that for some years to come readers will find it illuminating. It looks ahead to a time, not so very distant, when the average family income in the United States will be $10,000 a year (in dollars of 1967 purchasing power). It also, while forecasting growth in output and incomes, points to some generally overlooked considerations that may restrain the pace of growth, both in the economy as a whole and in particular markets.

Efforts to peer into the economic future tend to be quickly overtaken by obsolescence, but the chapters of this book have an extra ingredient that makes for durability: original analysis. The *Fortune* writers, researchers, editors, and economists whose work went into the chapters were not primarily trying to forecast what the gross national product or the market for cars or houses would be in any particular year. They were primarily trying to analyze and delineate trends and forces and patterns that will be affecting these and other aspects of the economy in years ahead. This kind of analysis is not quickly rendered obsolete by the passage of time or the appearance of more recent data. In each instance, the writer interviewed authorities in the field and consulted published estimates, but at the core of each chapter is a work of analysis. The projection are *Fortune*'s own, constructed anew from basic data.

Each chapter casts its own beam of light in its own way. The reader will find a diversity of approaches, styles, and even time periods. He will also find a recurrent (but not dominating) theme, a questioning whether demand in the private economy will be adequate over the next several years to fuel the kind of sustained boom that began in 1961 (and halted in a slowdown of growth in 1967). This theme, sounded in the first chapter, recurs in one variation or another in the chapters on population, autos, housing, and home goods, and in a muted way in the chapter on incomes. But the book is concerned with much more than this theme.

Wording has been altered here and there, but essentially the material appears in this book as it appeared in *Fortune*. No numbers have been altered, even in the instances where revised data have become available.*

Numerous members of *Fortune*'s staff share the responsibility and the credit for this book. William Bowen wrote Chapter 1 and served as editor of most of the other chapters; Lawrence A. Mayer wrote Chapters 2, 5, and 7; Jeremy Main, Chapter 3; Morris Cohen, Chapter 4; and Eleanore Carruth, Chapter 6. The following members of *Fortune*'s

---

* The following instances of revised data (none of which significantly affects any pattern or argument in the book) are noted for readers who may want to make use of particular figures. Chapter 1: the growth rate of gross national product in the years 1962–66 was subsequently adjusted upward, from 5.4 percent to 5.6 percent. Chapter 2: the birthrate for 1966 was adjusted downward, from 18.6 percent to 18.4 percent. Chapter 5: the home-goods share of disposable income in 1966, downward slightly, from 6 percent to 5.9 percent; color TV sales in 1966, were subsequently reported to have been closer to $2 billion than to $2.5 billion.

research staff assisted them: Marjorie Jack, Evelyn Benjamin, Jan Nagel Clarkson, Mary Gleason, Wyndham G. Robertson, and Edith Roper. The series also received inputs from *Fortune*'s economic staff, headed by Sanford S. Parker. Outside consultants made major contributions, which are noted in the appropriate chapters. Charts throughout the book are the work of Alexander Semenoick of *Fortune*'s art staff. Writers, researchers, and economists obtained information from literally scores of people outside *Fortune,* in private corporations, universities, trade associations, and government agencies. Thanks are hereby extended to all who helped.

The Editors of *Fortune*

1

The United States Economy Enters a New Era

THE GLORIOUS ECONOMIC SURGE of 1962-66 roared on so vigorously for so long that it tilted upward our expectations for the future. It is now generally recognized that the economy has slowed down a bit, but it is also widely assumed that after a brief sag the boom will get going again. Unfortunately, this expectation is likely to be disappointed. The 1962-66 boom was not a new kind of normality, but a result of special forces and circumstances. The economy was moving in a long cyclical upswing, and it was lifted along by an unsustainably rapid expansion of business investment, combined with an extraordinarily powerful demand for consumer goods. The next five years are likely to be very different.

No such clouded picture of the future appears in the armful of recently published long-range projections of the economy (for example, the Department of Labor's *Projections*

1

1970, and the just released study of "U.S. Economic Growth to 1975," prepared for the Joint Economic Committee of Congress). It has come to be standard procedure, inside and outside the United States government, for economists working up such projections to start out by assuming full employment—usually a 4-percent unemployment rate—in whatever year they are projecting. This assumption cuts an instant path through thickets of uncertainty. The projector calculates the potential output of the economy at full employment, and takes it for granted that aggregate demand will be present to match that supply. But it is precisely on the demand side that the main reasons for doubt arise about the economy's performance over the next several years.

Such projections, to be sure, are not meant to be taken as forecasts, but they often are so taken, for it is a natural inclination to suppose that the projector intends his assumptions to be realistic. The assumption that the economy will operate at full employment, however, is not based on any analysis of markets, consumption, or investment. To the extent that it has any link with reality at all, it rests upon another assumption, often left unstated: that the government can steer the economy into full employment. All the talk about the "managed economy"—sometimes abetted by the claims of the Washington managers themselves—has given a misleading picture of what federal action can accomplish. Strong economic growth (big wars aside) still depends upon forces in the private economy that government cannot entirely control.

In *Fortune*'s own look at the prospects for the years 1967-71, we consider the effects of government policy, but only as one of the factors at work in the economy. Subsequent chapters explore in detail some particular influences upon the economy, such as population trends, and some particular markets, such as housing and autos. This chapter considers basic developments that will affect economic growth in 1967-71. We take a five-year period because that seems about as far as it is possible to see ahead with some clarity. It also happens to be a span conveniently equal in length to the 1962-66 boom.

Looking five years into the economic future might seem an excessively hazardous undertaking with the Vietnam war on. Actually, however, the war has reached a stage where we can begin to see beyond it—in an economic sense, that is. In the past two years it has played a dominant—indeed explosive—role in the economy. The build-up may continue, but probably at a greatly moderated pace. Whether there is prolonged conflict or negotiated peace, Vietnam expenditures will no longer have a decisive effect upon the economy. Therefore it becomes all the more relevant to look at the normal peacetime sources of demand.

Over the past five years the United States gross national product (GNP) has grown at the rate of 5.4 percent a year in real terms. In the next five years, the best it can be expected to do is grow at about 4 percent. Over a long span of years, growth of real output is the combined result of three elemental factors: growth of the labor force, growth of the over-all productivity of the labor force, and a third one that links the other two. This third factor is the long-term decline in average weekly hours per worker (the work week gets shorter, vacations get longer). The economy cannot grow, in the long run, any faster than these three factors make possible. If you know their long-term trend rates of change, you can calculate the potential rate of GNP growth —the rate at which the economy would grow each year if it never wobbled.

Start with labor-force growth, which can be closely estimated from population figures: over the next five years the rate of increase will be approximately 1.7 percent a year. Then adjust this figure to allow for the decrease in average hours per worker. Of course, you don't *know* what this will be, but it is reasonable to assume that it will match the long-term rate of 0.4 percent a year. Subtracting this from 1.7 gives 1.3 percent as the rate at which total man-hours worked can be expected to grow. Then add 2.7 percent for the average year-to-year gain in productivity.* That comes to 4 percent.

In the 1962-66 period the economy performed quite a bit above its long-term potential. This was possible because in the preceding few years it had performed below its potential. In 1961 the nation was in a recession, with 6.7 percent of the labor force unemployed. On the upswing, the unemployment rate dropped below 6, then below 5, and in early

* The trend rate of productivity gain for the private economy is usually reckoned at 3.2 percent a year, but in calculating the potential rate of GNP growth it is necessary to adjust the figure downward, because the total labor force includes government workers, who produce no marketed output. It is a standard assumption that their productivity does not increase.

What Made the
Upswing Swing

Fig. 1. The extraordinary strength of the 1962-66 boom shows up vividly in these charts in the contrast between the wavy ups and downs before 1961 and the straight upward slope thereafter. Where the thrust for the 1962-66 boom came from is obvious in the steep and sustained climbs of business fixed investment and consumer purchases of goods. The consumer-goods boom included several component booms, notably in clothing (up 35 percent from 1961 to 1966), furniture and household equipment (60 percent), and, above all, automobiles (70 percent). Consumer spending on services continued on its smooth long-term growth curve, which appears to be virtually unaffected by year-to-year economic fluctuations. Despite the rising annual budgets, government purchases provided little upward push to the economy, growing much less rapidly than GNP. Federal purchases excluding defense and space show up as a narrow band on the chart because Washington's nondefense expenditures largely consist of transfer payments and grants to states rather than purchases of goods and services.

The three broad sectors charted here add up to about 95 percent of the economy. The remainder is made up of net change in business inventories, private housing, and net exports.

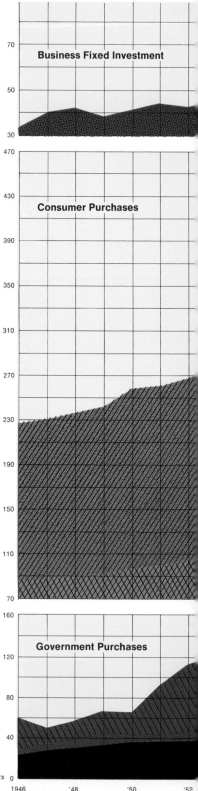

Billions of constant dollars

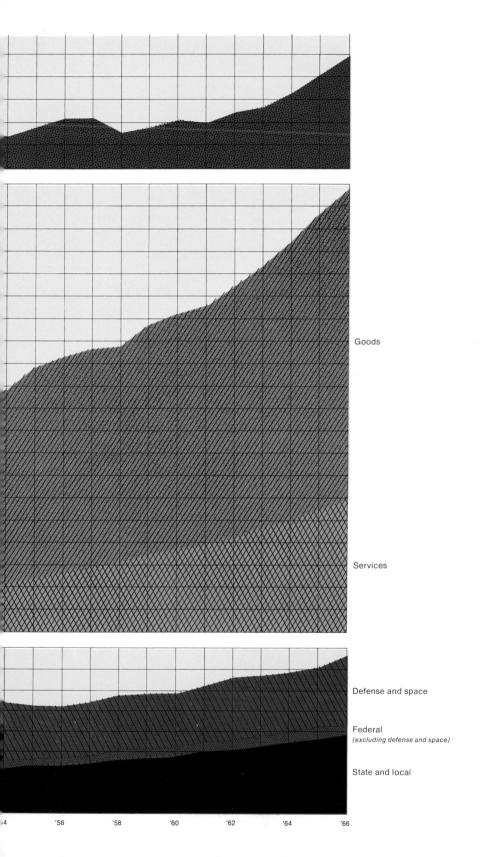

Goods

Services

Defense and space

Federal
(excluding defense and space)

State and local

'54   '56   '58   '60   '62   '64   '66

1966 finally reached 4 percent, the administration's "interim" full-employment goal. With unemployment declining and overtime replacing short weeks, growth in total man-hours leaped far ahead of the long-term rate. Productivity gains also exceeded the norm, as usually happens in the early stages of an economic upturn.

With the economy at full employment, however, there is no reserve of jobless workers to provide an extra push to output. From 1967 on, even if it should remain at full employment, the economy cannot do better over a span of years than grow at the 4 percent potential rate determined by basic noncyclical factors—though of course the rate may vary from one year to the next.

This 4-percent figure is bad news only if you suppose the rates of the recent past to be normal. By any long-view standard, 4-percent-a-year growth in real GNP would be an exceedingly pleasant prospect. Over the first half of this century, real GNP grew at a rate of only 3 percent. Even with the postwar improvement in year-to-year productivity gains, the long-term growth rate since the end of World War II has amounted to about 3.6 percent. In the period we are now entering, the potential growth rate will be considerably higher than that because the labor force will be growing faster. During the 1950s and early 1960s it grew at an average of 1.3 percent a year. From 1967 on, into the late 1970s, the rate will be 0.4 percent higher, reflecting the high birth rates of the postwar baby boom.

From the abundant base at which the economy is now operating, moreover, 4-percent growth over the next five years would mount up to an immense number of dollars. In constant 1966 dollars, 1971 GNP would amount to $900 billion. The addition to GNP over the five-year period would come to $160 billion, only $12 billion less than the amount added to GNP by the 1962-66 boom. That's hardly austerity.

But that 4 percent, it is important to note, represents the potential rate, the best the economy *can* do. What really matters is how near its potential it *will* perform.

To begin with, there is some question whether an economy at full employment can keep on registering normal year-to-year productivity gains. There is little experience to go on. But it is evident that productivity gains tend to dwindle as the economy approaches full employment—late deliveries slow up production, plant discipline loosens, experienced workers are diverted to train inexperienced newcomers. In 1956, for example, unemployment declined to 4.2 percent and productivity gained a next-to-nothing 0.1 percent. In the latest upswing, productivity gains ran above the postwar trend in 1962-64, but then slipped below it in 1965 and 1966.

Also, there has so far proved to be a troubling conflict between full employment and price stability. In the early sixties the consumer price index edged up about 1.2 percent a year, a rate of creep that we have come to accept as "stability." (With wages in the service sector persistently rising faster than productivity, the consumer price index creeps even when wholesale prices remain stable.) But in 1966, with the economy at full employment, the index went up 3.3 percent (from December 1965 to December 1966). And inflation ran at that worrisome rate in spite of strenuous administration efforts to hold back prices by intervening directly in business pricing decisions. That 3.3 percent rise in consumer prices, moreover, did not fully measure the inflationary momentum that was generated in the economy, for there was a carry-over of cost-push in 1967 as labor got extra wage increases to make up for the 1966 rise in living costs. In the end, inflation tends to undermine full employment, first by causing distortions in the economy, and second by inviting counterinflationary policies, such as monetary restraints, which slow down the pace of economic activity.

The crucial question for the next five years, however, is whether there will be enough push of *demand* to keep the economy growing at its full employment potential. The powerful driving force in the 1962-66 upswing was a roaring boom in capital investment. In the coming period, business investment can hardly be expected to repeat its performance. Fixed investment (i.e., in plant and equipment) expanded much faster than GNP—at an extraordinary rate of 9.7 percent a year. It is elementary that fixed investment cannot continue indefinitely to expand at a faster rate than GNP; productive capacity cannot go on growing faster than demand for what the capacity produces. The dollar amount of business fixed investment will not necessarily decline from the exuberant $79.3 billion of 1966, but the rate of year-to-year increase will have to decline, and sharply.

It is doubtful, indeed, whether fixed investment can grow

even as fast as GNP during the next several years. This doubt arises because at the level to which it climbed in 1966 fixed capital investment represented 10.7 percent of GNP, extraordinarily high by the standards of the postwar years. In 1948, when business was making up for the long stretch of underinvestment during the depression and the war, fixed investment amounted to 11.3 percent of GNP. But that was clearly abnormal, and after 1948 the percentage never topped 10.2 until 1966. It may not slip all the way back to the 9.5-percent average of 1948-64, but slip it almost certainly will. Capital investment is currently adding capacity faster than the economy can grow over the long term. As investment gets back to a more normal level, the extra push it has been giving the economy will disappear.

The other driving force in the recent boom, consumer demand, will continue to contribute to the economy's growth, but the question is how strongly. The intensity of consumer demand over a span of time depends in part on such unpredictable elements as changes in public mood and introductions of new products. So any forecast has to be tempered with a large admixture of uncertainty.

One unfavorable omen is that consumers piled up quite a lot of debt during the 1962-66 upswing. A useful way to measure this debt is against the nation's total disposable income (the money people have to spend after paying taxes). Consumer credit outstanding rose from 16 percent of total disposable income in 1961 to nearly 19 percent in 1966. Consumers also spent a lot of extra cash obtained through mortgage refinancings, which drew down home-owners' equities by many billions of dollars in 1962-65 (tight money brought the practice to a halt last year). All this was reflected in a subnormal rate of net personal saving in the economy as a whole. This rate, as reckoned by the Department of Commerce, is the percentage of total disposable income left over after subtraction of total personal outlays. It averaged 6 percent in the years 1957-61, and during the early fifties it was considerably higher than that. Over the past five years the rate averaged 5.4 percent; in 1966 it was 5.3.

The debt load may impose some restraint upon consumer demand in the years ahead. It seems unlikely that home-owners' equities will be thinned down in the next five years

The Reversing Pyramid of Income

Fig. 2. United States consumer markets of the future will increasingly be dominated by the effects of the powerful ongoing trend illustrated in these charts—the reversal of the income pyramid that has been typical of human societies through the centuries. To cancel out inflation, the charts show the changing distribution of income in constant 1965 dollars.

Seen in perspective, the evolutionary shift in the income structure seems revolutionary in its cumulative effect. In 1950 three out of five families had incomes of less than $5,000, and only one in five had an income of $7,000 or more. By 1965, virtually half of all families had incomes of $7,000 or more, and only one-third were below $5,000. In the years ahead, the $7,000-or-more families will make up an increasing majority. By 1970, or soon after, $10,000-or-more families will outnumber those with incomes of less than $5,000.

Distribution of families by income group *(in constant dollars)*

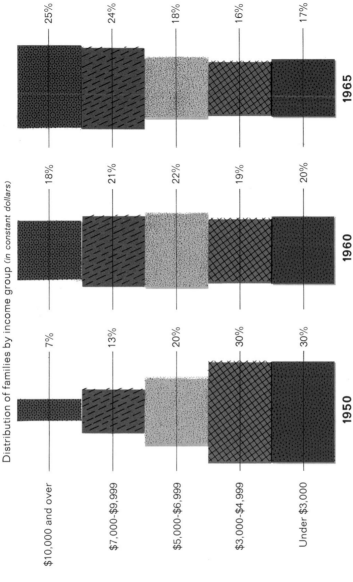

	1950	1960	1965
$10,000 and over	7%	18%	25%
$7,000–$9,999	13%	21%	24%
$5,000–$6,999	20%	22%	18%
$3,000–$4,999	30%	19%	16%
Under $3,000	30%	20%	17%

as much as in the past five, or that consumer credit will expand as fast relative to disposable income. To the extent that consumers add debt less rapidly, they will have that much less extra money to spend.

One consideration often cited as favorable for consumer markets is the population trend. Since formations of new households and births of first children are powerful generators of demand, it has been widely assumed that rapid increase in the numbers of people in their twenties would bring rapid increase in consumer demand. And so it will, in time. But there are lags between the time these young people enter the labor force and the time they marry and have children. The labor force has already begun to grow rapidly, but the extra impetus of consumer demand will be delayed.

The great increase in the numbers of people in their twenties may have other adverse economic effects. Professor Richard A. Easterlin of the University of Pennsylvania has pointed out that it will tend to narrow their opportunities as members of the labor force. Born in low-birth-rate years, the people who came into their twenties during the 1950s and 1960s benefited from their relative scarcity. Now relative scarcity is turning into relative abundance. From the mid-1950s through the early 1960s, people in their twenties were considerably less numerous than people in their thirties; by 1971, people in their twenties will outnumber those in their thirties, seven to five. Being so much more numerous, young people will have to compete harder for good jobs and promotions than did their counterparts in the 1950s and early 1960s. Accordingly, they may be less confident about their future as earners and providers, more reluctant to assume family responsibilities, less willing and less able to take on a lot of consumer debt early in their working lives.

Such considerations about the prospective vigor of demand are pretty lightly dismissed nowadays, for it has come to be widely assumed that government will make up for any lags in the private economy. And the Great Society rhetoric of recent years does indeed lend credence to the idea. A leap of aims so large that it has shifted orders of magnitude is evident in formulations of national goals ("an end to poverty," "a total program for human betterment"). In campus radicalism, this expansion of public goals is typically spoken of as if it constituted an overdue recognition of national failure. But it is more perceptive to see the new grandiosity as a sign of national success, for as the philosopher Alfred North Whitehead observed, "Vigorous societies harbor a certain extravagance of objectives. . . ." It is a misreading of what has happened to think it happened because President Johnson raised up a banner with the vague device "Great Society." The expansion of goals has resulted from basic social realities. Growing national wealth has made it possible to conceive of very large social undertakings. Rising levels of education have brought enlargements of sympathies, widenings of horizons. And various public problems have come to seem very much more pressing than they seemed in the fifties.

The new "extravagance of objectives" obviously implies quite a few billions of additional federal expenditures over the next several years. Some of the Great Society legislation enacted so far is open-ended, in the sense that large expansions of funds could be voted by Congress without substantial amendments. A member of the President's cabinet once remarked that the Demonstration Cities Act, funded for only $11 million in fiscal 1967, had "opened the door to billions." Indeed, the once far-out term "trillion" has been heard in the land. After listening to New York's Mayor John V. Lindsay testify on his city's need for additional federal funds, Senator Robert F. Kennedy noted that if all cities needed similar federal aid in proportion to population, the ten-year total would come to a trillion dollars. That's one-third again as much as the nation's entire GNP in 1966.

Still, it is far from clear that all this is going to provide a powerful surge of economic demand over the five-year span we are considering. Practical influences will restrain the translation of grandiose goals into commensurately grandiose expenditures. And even if federal spending does rise a great deal, that will not necessarily have the stimulating effect that some people blithely assume.

To begin with, there are the difficulties of designing programs that can meet reasonable standards of cost effectiveness. The advent of large social goals has found us conspicuously short of clear, thought-out designs for achieving them. There is an awareness in Washington, even among men committed to eventual large expansions of social-goal expenditures, that a lot of advance thinking is called for. John W. Gardner, who as Secretary of Health, Education, and Welfare administered most of the administration's Great Society programs, once remarked: "The need for money is less acute than the need for new ways to use it." Advocates of speed in the expansion of Great Society undertakings often argue that the United States can "afford" greater expenditures for such goals as ending poverty. But, as economist Milton Friedman has pointed out, agreement that the nation can "afford" some particular government program still leaves a question of whether the program is worth the money. Legislators and their taxpaying constituents will be reluctant to support large increases in outlays for programs that do not appear to be producing results commensurate with their costs.

To a great extent, moreover, government expenditures for social-goal programs take the form of transfer payments, which result in relatively small net additions to demand in the economy. Government's principal way of raising the incomes of the poor or near poor is to pay them money either directly (public assistance, aid to dependent children, social security) or indirectly (medicare, rent supplements). A growing body of opinion argues for much larger money payments to the poor through a "negative income tax," a guaranteed annual income, or some other new form of redistribution. In any case, such transfers only shuffle money around: the recipients have more to spend, but taxpayers have that much less. The redistribution adds to total consumer purchases only in that money is shifted from persons who collectively would have saved a significant percentage of it to other persons who collectively save very little of it. If the difference in saving amounted to 10 percent of the total transferred, then government would have to redistribute $10 billion to add $1 billion to consumer purchases. Clearly, no great stimulus to the economy can be expected from this direction.

Far more significant is what happens to government purchases of goods and services. This is the only category of government expenditures that shows up as a component of GNP in the national income and product accounts published by the Department of Commerce. It includes the pay of government employees and purchases from the private economy.

From the size of the federal budget, you might suppose that federal purchases amount to a lot more than total state and local government purchases. They don't. As a share of

GNP, federal purchases declined from 14.7 percent in 1954 to 10.4 percent in 1966. State and local purchases, in contrast, grew from 8.9 percent of GNP to 10.3, ending up neck and neck with the federal total.

There are reasons to believe, however, that over the next five years state and local purchases will grow less briskly than in the fifties and early sixties. Much of state and local government consists in providing services and facilities for people (trash collection, traffic control), and the costs grow with growth of population. The slower population growth resulting from the birth-rate decline of recent years will bring some easing here. In particular, needs for additional school facilities will become less pressing, for the school-age population will be increasing at a much slower rate than during the early sixties—1.2 percent a year instead of 3. Also, medicare will reduce pressure for expansion of public hospital facilities, a substantial item.

A team of George Washington University economists has made a detailed study of prospective state and local purchases in 1970 and concluded that they will grow at "a declining rate" over the next several years. For 1970 they projected purchases equivalent to $91.5 billion in 1966 dollars. That would mean an increase of $15.4 billion over actual 1966 purchases, and a growth rate of 4.7 percent a year. From 1962 through 1966, state and local purchases expanded at a constant-dollar rate of 5.6 percent a year.

Moderate growth in state and local purchases is also foreseen in a recent study of "State and Local Public Facility Needs and Financing," prepared for the congressional subcommittee on economic progress. This massive report incorporates separate analyses, done by experts, of forty-two distinct sectors, ranging from "Public Water Supply Systems" (authored by the American Waterworks Association) to "Jails and Prisons" (by the Federal Bureau of Prisons). The consolidated projections show state and local "expenditures for structures and equipment" advancing at a rate of 4.6 percent a year from 1965 to 1975. The projections, the report notes, "would appear to be at odds with predictions that growing demands on state and local governments for public services will require some reallocation of fiscal resources."

As for federal purchases, the biggest segment by far is defense, and in a five-year perspective, contraction of defense purchases seems much more likely than expansion. In one way or another, whether through negotiated settlement or fade-out, large-scale combat operations in Vietnam will certainly come to an end within the next few years.

The resulting fall-off in defense spending, however, will be much less steep than is generally supposed. The total armed forces have been expanded by 700,000 because of Vietnam, and it will take a year or more after the war ends to get back to former levels. The decline in defense purchases will be tempered, also, by expenditures to replenish military inventories and to catch up on projects that the Defense Department has deferred or stretched out—military construction at home, advanced research and development projects, re-equipment of Army units outside Vietnam. And within a few years the United States may be spending a couple of billion a year on an antimissile system. With these new costs partly offsetting the drop in war costs, 1971 defense purchases may well run as high as 1966's $60 billion. Still that would mean a decline of several billion from the total in 1967.

Space purchases in 1966 came to around $6 billion, but with Apollo development costs past their peak, they will be declining in the next couple of years. They will go up again later on if Congress authorizes new space undertakings, but even so, space purchases in 1971 will not be much larger than in 1966.

That leaves federal purchases other than for defense and space. This segment of government purchases showed no growth at all in 1962-66—shrank a bit, in fact. Nondefense, nonspace *expenditures* increased over that span, of course, from $52 billion to $74 billion, but the additional funds went out mostly in transfer payments and in grants to the states. With all the Great Society stir around, it would be unrealistic to assume no widening at all in this band of federal purchases over the next five years, but it would also be unrealistic to expect it to widen by many billions.

It can hardly be assumed, then, that expansion of total government purchases will make up for any lags in the vigor of private demand in the years ahead. With slacking off in capital investment and consumer demand in prospect, the outlook for growth of total government purchases does not appear to support expectations of sustained full employment.

Of course, the administration will presumably *try* to keep

the economy near full employment and growing at close to a 4-percent rate. It is bound by the Employment Act of 1946 to "promote maximum employment, production, and purchasing power," and this obligation has been powerfully reinforced over the years by an accumulation of official utterances involving the administration's prestige with the performance of the economy. But the yet-to-be-answered question is whether the federal government *can* keep the economy growing at its potential rate when demand in the private economy is slack.

If demand gets painfully slack, the government can try to inflate demand by cutting taxes or increasing its own expenditures. But either course, or a mixture of both, entails widening budget deficits. Big deficits tighten money markets (government has to borrow *somewhere*), and the resulting upward push in interest rates works against expansion of private demand. And neither tax reduction nor increase in government spending will necessarily bring quick results, in terms of demand in the private economy, or even slow results that are commensurate with the increase in deficits. The strong growth that followed the tax cuts enacted in 1964 did not prove the efficacy of government management, for the economy was then riding on the up side of a capital-investment cycle. To keep the economy booming after the topping out of an investment cycle will be a more difficult and less certain undertaking.

These considerations about private demand and government limitations do not add up, and are not meant to add up, to an ironclad conclusion that aggregate demand will be too sluggish to sustain vigorous growth. In an economy so big and so dynamic, many possibilities are open. Favorable developments may bring substantial enlargements of demand from any of several directions.

Progress from vague social-goal aspirations to well-designed programs of action may proceed faster than now seems probable. In particular, the pervasive concern about the cities may lead to some effective combination of public and private resources for rebuilding on a grand scale.

Slackness in capital investment to expand capacity may be largely offset by an increase in "deepening" investment to improve efficiency and lower costs. Technological innovations would favor this kind of investment.

Introduction of new products may enlarge consumer demand. Many new consumer products only displace other products (Corfam instead of leather in shoes, cordless appliances instead of plug-in counterparts), but now and then a product comes along, TV, for example, and creates demand that wasn't there before. Such consumer products, in turn, engender new capital investment to make and market them.

One large sector of the economy that provided no lift at all to demand in recent years may be providing a great deal in the next several years. That is housing. The dollar value of new "residential structures," as it is called in the national income and product accounts, rose from $26 billion in 1961 to $30 billion in 1963, but then sagged back to $26 billion in 1966. Housing has nowhere to go but up, and it will probably go up a lot. New household formations, of course, swell demand for housing, and household formations will be increasing at an accelerating pace as those postwar babies come of age. And greatly enlarged demand for housing brings demand for furniture and appliances.

Looking ahead beyond five years, to the middle 1970s, it is possible to discern potentialities for invigorated demand and accelerated growth. Evolution of new technologies and new ways of thinking systematically about the future may result in, among other things, an increase in over-all economic efficiency; an array of products novel enough to create new demand for both producer and consumer goods; an improved capacity to translate social aspirations into effective action.

During the next five years or so, however, *visible* effects may be rather faint. It takes time to move from technological innovations to marketable new products, and it takes time also for new ways of thinking to produce politically acceptable designs for action.

But more will have happened by 1971 than will meet the eye. During the next several years some of the most important new products will not be counted in the national income and product tabulations. These new products will be new concepts, plans, and formulations that will gradually diminish the gap between our aspirations to achieve a greater society and our dim notions of how to achieve it—or even of what it will be like when we do.

2

Why the United States Population Isn't Exploding

WHILE MOST PEOPLE have been concerned about the great world-wide population explosion, some Americans have become aware of—and concerned about—the curious decline in the rate of population growth in the United States. To be sure, this country passed the 200-million mark in 1967. And, of course, the growth rate has declined from a high level: from 1946 to 1961 population growth averaged 1.7 percent a year, an extraordinary rate for a major industrial nation to sustain. Nevertheless, the change since 1961 has been extraordinary too; in a recent twelve-month period the rate came to only 1.1 percent. The United States was adding about 3 million people a year during the 1950s; in 1966 the figure was only a little more than 2 million.

The professional demographers, who have attentively noted this decline, appear to have two quite different notions about it. Some believe that the decline principally reflects a desire of young women to have children somewhat later in life than women had them in the 1950s: the births are being postponed but will be made up later. But most demographers are coming to another view. They suspect that more than a change in the timing of births is involved, that younger couples want to have fewer children.

Both sides in this argument agree that the rate of growth will be turning back up fairly soon, for the children of the postwar baby boom are themselves becoming old enough to marry and have children. What is involved, then, is a matter of degree: how *much* growth may we anticipate? The answer to this question is an important matter—as two different Census Bureau projections suggest. The bureau's "B" (medium high) projection assumes that women will continue to time their child-bearing differently but not try to reduce family size: it shows about 5,400,000 births in the United States in 1975. The "C" (medium low) projection assumes that family size is coming down: it shows 4,700,000 births in 1975.

A sizable number of businessmen, in markets ranging from toys and baby food to houses and appliances, have been waiting restlessly for the new wave of marriages and births to power the economy in the 1970s. Thus the demographers' disagreements may be translated into differing expectations about the pace of growth in different markets. But before looking at this matter more closely, it will pay to review briefly the course of population trends in the postwar years.

The trends have frequently discomfited the Census Bureau, whose projections have been trailing the events of the past two decades. As population continued to climb rapidly after 1947, the bureau had to keep revising its projections upward. Projections about future growth were at their highest in 1958, just when actual growth had passed its crest, and they have been chasing the facts back down ever since. Back in 1958 the bureau's "B" projection, the one then most widely used in market research, anticipated a population of 236,-400,000 by 1975. Since 1958 the "B" projection has twice been revised downward, yet its assumptions seemed, in 1967, unduly optimistic to many marketing men, and the projection being fed into most business plans for the future is the Census "C." This yields a population in 1975 of 219,400,000

—17 million less than was thought most probable in 1958. Thus businessmen generally are looking forward to only about half the addition to population that they once expected to take place between 1967 and 1975.

There is no doubt that these reduced expectations are primarily related to the drop in births; other influences on population growth have been negligible. The death rate has remained stable, at 9.4 per thousand, for about a decade. (An improved record in combating infectious diseases has offset higher death rates for cancer, heart trouble, diabetes, cirrhosis of the liver, accidents, and violence.) The effect of immigration is also minor, although immigration has increased since Congress liberalized the entry requirements in 1965. Census population projections now make an annual allowance of 400,000 for net immigration, up from 300,000 a few years ago.

But the fall-off in births has been spectacular. They hit a peak of 4,308,000 in 1957 and stayed near that mark for several years. Thereafter the totals gradually slipped, to 4,027,000 in 1964; and then they slipped more rapidly, to 3,629,000 in 1966. Birth *rates*, of course, declined more rapidly still, because the population base was growing all the while. The so-called crude rate, which relates total births to the total population, fell from 25.3 per thousand in 1957 to 18.6 in 1966. On the face of the matter, this is an amazingly low level. It has not been matched in the United States since the depths of the depression (and never before then), and it was, of course, registered in a period of tremendous prosperity. The "C" projection implies that the crude rate in 1975 would still be a relatively modest 21.3 per thousand.

To understand what is happening, it is helpful to turn from the crude rate to a more sophisticated measure, the "total fertility rate." This reflects the rates at which, in any given year, women of different ages bear children; the total fertility rate is the sum of all these "age-specific rates." The rate shot up to a high level after World War II, and then steadily rose further during the early 1950s. By 1957 it had reached the extraordinary level of 3,724 per thousand women aged fourteen to forty-nine—i.e., in that year women between the ages of fourteen and forty-nine were building families at a rate which, if sustained, would have given them an average of 3.7 children each by the end of their child-bearing years. All demographers recognized the 1957 fertility rate as extraordinary and unsustainable. No cohort of women (the term refers to all those born in any particular year) had actually completed families that large in several decades; the last cohort that averaged as many as 3.7 children was that born in 1876. What is more, the responses to an extensive survey carried out in 1955 showed that married women on the average expected only a little more than three children.

It was evident that several forces were temporarily inflating fertility in 1957. Younger women were getting married earlier and having children sooner after marriage. Meanwhile, older women were also raising the rate by their efforts to catch up on child-bearing that had been delayed, first by the depression and then by the war. On balance, it seemed likely that about 20 percent of that 1957 fertility rate was unsustainable. With more normal timing of births, the totals would soon decline, and so would the crude birth rate. Then, went the standard forecast, in the mid-1960s, as the huge baby crops of 1946 and the following years began to reach the marriageable ages, all of the birth statistics would turn up and a tremendous new population boom would get under way.

These forecasts have already been proved wrong in some respects and have come to seem shaky in others. No one anticipated how steep the decline would be or how long it would last. The Census projections generally assumed that the turnaround would take place about 1964. The lowest of several Census projections prepared in that year estimated 3,928,000 births in the year ending June 30, 1967. Even this low estimate now seems excessive by 300,000. Worst of all, for the forecasters, is the mounting evidence that the decline may be related to a desire for smaller families—which, if the evidence is confirmed, would make the next boom not so tremendous after all.

What happened? First, *which* women have had fewer children than expected? Arthur A. Campbell of the National Center for Health Statistics has shed some light on this matter. He has shown that the high fertility rates of the late 1950s were inflated more by births ahead of schedule than by the catch-up of postponed births. (His concept of

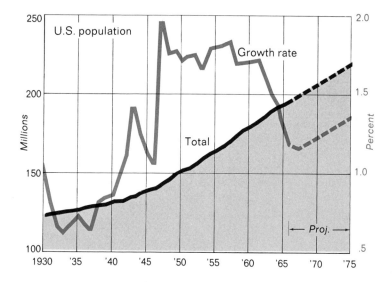

Fig. 3. The United States population grew by an average of 1.7 percent in the fifteen years after World War II—a level not sustained by any other advanced nations except Canada, Australia, and New Zealand, all of which depended for much of the growth on heavy immigration. Recently, a decline in births has cut the United States rate to little more than 1 percent—about average for an advanced nation these days. The growth rate will recover somewhat from now on, even on the Census "medium low" projection charted here.

Women in their early twenties are having fewer children...

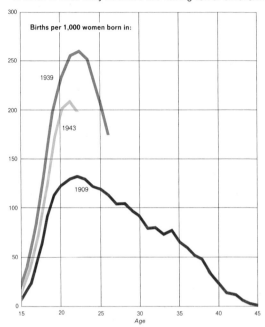

...and so birth rates are down now...

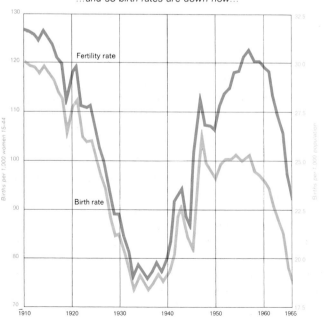

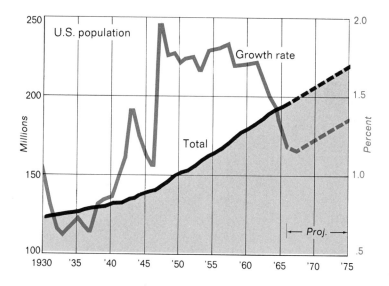

Fig. 3. The United States population grew by an average of 1.7 percent in the fifteen years after World War II—a level not sustained by any other advanced nations except Canada, Australia, and New Zealand, all of which depended for much of the growth on heavy immigration. Recently, a decline in births has cut the United States rate to little more than 1 percent—about average for an advanced nation these days. The growth rate will recover somewhat from now on, even on the Census "medium low" projection charted here.

"normal" timing was derived from the experience of all women born between 1901 and 1945.) He has also shown that in 1960-64, when the total fertility rate was at a reduced but still high level, young women were continuing to have children abnormally early. He concluded in 1965 that they would soon have to cut back drastically, and that the rate, which had been averaging around 3,450 births per thousand women, would thereupon fall below the norm to something like 2,800 in 1965-69. That seems to be just what has been happening; births have fallen precipitously, and the annual rate for the first few months of 1967 was actually about 2,750. In other words, the fall-off in births can be related largely to a new pattern among younger women, who are either postponing their children or planning fewer of them —but in any case were having fewer in 1967.

This new pattern among young women emerged quite suddenly, as can be seen in the experience of girls born only four years apart. Those born in 1939 seem to have set the all-time record for early child-bearing in the United States. By twenty-three they had already averaged 1.23 children apiece. The girls born in 1943 had a distinctly lower average, with only 1.05 children at the same age. (See Figs. 4, 5, and 6.) In general, among all the girls born in the 1940s, each yearly group seems to be bearing children at a slightly slower pace than its predecessor.

One reason for this decline appears to be what is sometimes whimsically referred to as the "marriage squeeze." The term refers principally to the curious plight of girls who were born in the suddenly swollen baby crops of 1946-48. They are now of an age when American girls normally expect to get married. However, American girls also normally expect to marry men two or three years older than themselves; and, unfortunately, good men are especially hard to find for girls in those cohorts of 1946-48 because the male cohorts of 1943-45 were much smaller. The squeeze is at its most intense right now, but in some degree the problem has been affecting young women for several years and it will persist well into the 1970s. It is hard to assess the importance of the marriage squeeze, but its effect is visible in statistics showing that, while the median age of marriage for men has remained stable, the age for women has gone up slightly (to 20.5 years). A computer analysis by Census indicates that this rise could be accounted for by the marriage squeeze. There is no evidence, incidentally, that the Vietnam war and the draft have affected marriage rates among younger Americans.

If it is clear that the fall-off in births can be ascribed primarily to new patterns among younger women, it is not so clear which social or economic groups are mainly involved. The decrease has apparently been quite pervasive, however. It shows up in every state of the union and among Negroes as well as whites.

Taking whites alone, however, it is reasonable to suspect that Roman Catholics may have contributed disproportionately to the decline. A major survey of birth-control practices in the United States, made by Professor Norman B. Ryder of the University of Wisconsin and Professor Charles F. Westoff of Princeton, has shown that in 1965 some 53 percent of Catholic couples were using contraceptive methods not sanctioned by the Church—up from 30 percent in 1955. The same study reported that even among devout Catholic women (defined as those who go to Mass at least once a week), 44 percent were not following Catholic teaching on contraception in 1965. (Among the nondevout the figure was 74 percent.) However, for those who regard increased Catholic acceptance of birth control as a major cause of lower birth rates, there is another statistic that somewhat clouds the picture: birth rates in the northeastern states (45 percent Catholic) have fallen no more than they have in the southern states (14 percent Catholic).

In any event, the main question about the reduced births is not who's doing the reducing but what these young parents have in mind. Are they simply postponing births or are they in the process of curtailing the ultimate size of their families? Judith Blake of the University of California at Berkeley is one eminent demographer who believes that the data suggest no more than a change in timing patterns; she believes that births have only been delayed and that they will be made up. She is clearly in the minority. A paper by Ronald Freedman and some of his colleagues at the University of Michigan suggests that "postponement of births may be a first step toward revising expectations downward. We have some evidence that expectations are revised downward rather quickly as time elapses without a pregnancy."

Women in their early twenties are having fewer children...

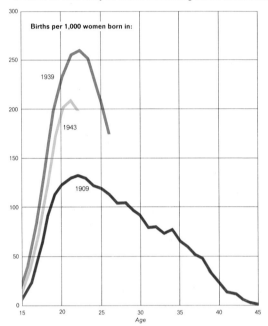

...and so birth rates are down now...

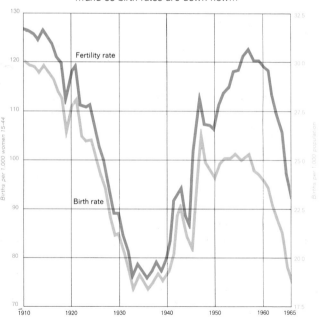

...but total births are about to turn up.

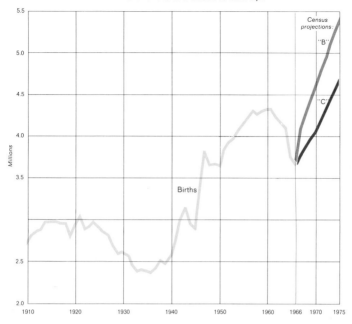

Fig. 4 (upper left). Women born in 1943 have had fewer children than women born in 1939 had at the same ages. The 1939 group had so many so soon that their rate of child-bearing later dropped precipitously. Still, on the average, they will wind up with about one child more than the women of 1909, who, affected by depression and war, averaged only 2.2 each—the least for any age group in United States history. The class of 1943 seems to be aiming for families somewhere between these two extremes. **Fig. 5 (left).** The main reason for those sharply declining birth rates has been a reduction in child-bearing among younger women. The conventional or "crude" birth rate (births compared to total population) is at depression levels. The fertility rate, a somewhat more refined measure (births compared to all women in the child-bearing ages), remains above depression levels because there are now relatively fewer women aged fifteen to forty-four. **Fig. 6 (upper right).** The declining birth rates have meant a declining number of births in recent years. However, births (and birth rates too) are virtually certain to turn up just about now because the many children born at the end of the war are themselves now entering the main child-bearing ages. On the medium-low "C," which is becoming the most widely used of the Census Bureau's current projections, the record 4,300,000 births of 1957 won't be equaled again until 1972.

Those who believe that births are only being delayed can point to a hard piece of evidence. It consists of surveys, taken over a number of years, which persistently indicate that married women expect an average of about 3.2 children. Such surveys have hitherto proved reliable. However, they are certainly not conclusive, and they seem, on balance, less compelling than certain other data that do point to smaller families.

One piece of evidence has to do with Negro families. Negro births have fallen somewhat less than white births, but Negroes, who are more likely to have large families, are cutting back the most on having *very* large families (five or more children). There is also the impact of new birth-control methods on both Negroes and whites. According to a 1960 study, 37 percent of all white couples had at least one child whose time of arrival was unplanned, while another 17 percent had more children than they wanted. The corresponding figures for Negro couples are higher. Obviously, any change that helps women to time pregnancies will also work to space out births and so tend to curtail the total number of births. This is precisely the role of "the pill," the now readily available oral contraceptive.

The pill is now the most widely used method of contraception in the United States. It is more effective than any other method, affording nearly 100 percent protection against unwanted pregnancies to the large majority of women who can use it. (Some women are bothered by side effects.) Its effectiveness is still substantial even when its users skip an occasional tablet in the monthly cycle. There is evidence that the pill has helped swing Roman Catholics to the practice of contraception, even though surveys have shown Catholics wanting more children than Protestants do. (White Catholic women have generally anticipated an average of 3.7 children, compared to 2.9 for white Protestants.) There is also evidence that the pill has encouraged the new generation of young women to control births effectively right from marriage; previously, many young couples used contraceptives irregularly, or not until after children had been born. The availability of oral contraceptives has been largely responsible for raising the proportion of couples using birth control from 79 percent in 1960 to nearly 85 in late 1965.

Right now it seems likely that about 6 million women

are using the pill (out of 48 million women between fourteen and forty-nine). Among married women eighteen to thirty-nine, the group primarily "at risk," as demographers put it, the proportion of current users may be nearing one-third and is still climbing.

One reason to expect use of the pill to keep on climbing is that younger women have accepted the pill more readily than older women. It is most popular among women under twenty-five, and as they grow older they will be replacing the generation currently thirty-five to forty-four years old, which has comparatively few users. Rising educational attainment will also work to expand use of the pill: rates of use by women who have completed high school and college are, respectively, double and triple those of women who have gone only to elementary school. Though fewer Negroes than whites use the pill, this largely reflects the difference in schooling; use is almost the same at the same levels of education.

Another reason for anticipating greater use of the pill is that the government has begun to support family planning —and family planning, in practice, frequently means the pill. There is a growing conviction that any successful war on poverty must include some kind of program to help women in large and destitute families prevent births they do not want, and the pill has made many such programs feasible. In 1962 public family-planning services were operating in only thirteen states; today there are at least minimal programs in forty-five states, serving about 350,000 women. Some of them have support from Washington—the Department of Health, Education, and Welfare now budgets $5 million for direct services, counseling, and information— and the programs are a good bet to grow.

In addition to these public programs, centers privately financed and run by Planned Parenthood-World Population are serving another 250,000 low-income women. Planned Parenthood estimates that there are 5 million women eighteen to forty-four who are medically indigent and might want the kind of service offered by the state programs and its own; all together, only about 12 percent of these women are being reached now.

The present pill is plainly only the first of a long line of new birth-control devices. On the horizon are a single tablet for an entire menstrual cycle; a pill that will not suppress ovulation (and thus possibly will avoid Catholic censure); oral contraceptives for males; and a capsule that could be implanted under the skin and for twenty years slowly leak a hormone that suppresses fertility (the capsule could be removed whenever a child is wanted). As such improvements come along, they will make contraception easier and further reduce "accidents."

The pill's manifest capabilities have led some to conclude that the entire decline in the birth rate can be attributed to it. That is grossly overstating the case, however; the decline, we have seen, began in 1958, and the pill was not in widespread use for several years after that. How much of the recent decline *can* be attributed to the pill? Some demographers would say perhaps 25 percent in the past two years. And plainly the new availability of birth-control techniques would not have had so much impact if a lot of people had not wanted to limit the number of their children for one reason or another. One powerful reason is the demonstrably rising cost of rearing children. It is increasingly desirable to provide them with good educations—and the cost of good educations is increasing. The Institute of Life Insurance says that it costs the average family $23,000 to raise a child to college age, and that college itself can then easily cost another $10,000. On this reckoning, three children mean a burden of about $100,000; one less would lighten the load by $33,000. Some couples that start out postponing a child end up deciding not to have it after all: while they're waiting, they get used to high living standards, and they may become more and more reluctant to reduce the standards by enlarging the family. And as they have postponed having children, many wives have been able to find interests and careers away from home; the increased availability of interesting jobs has surely helped some women decide against an extra child. "Who," a Census Bureau official remarked recently, "wants to go to PTA meetings forever?"

Some scholars have cited the strains and tensions of a mass society as forces working, subtly, against child-bearing. Philip M. Hauser, a professor of sociology at the University of Chicago, has put forward the view that as Americans become more and more concerned about the crowded conditions of their lives, even families able to afford many children will be under social pressures not to have them. "Even Bobby Kennedy," Hauser has said, "is creating kids who will interfere with my kids' air, water, and commuting space."

There are other subtle incentives at work to reduce the desire for large families. In a noteworthy series of papers that straddle demography and economics, Richard A. Easterlin, professor of economics at the University of Pennsylvania, has supplied one comprehensive explanation of our seemingly erratic postwar birth rates.

The key to the matter, Easterlin says, has been the ideas that young people have about the standards of living they need when they are married and have children, and their expectations about their ability to command these standards in the labor market. Birth rates fell rapidly in the 1920s and 1930s; thus there were comparatively few youngsters looking for jobs just after World War II, and they commanded exceptionally good wages. He also observes that the postwar generation was additionally fortunate: better equipped than their elders because high-school education had become widespread as they were growing up, these young people were able to move rapidly into better jobs than their parents had held. Meanwhile, their living-standard aspirations were modest because their tastes had been formed in households affected by the depression. Thus they felt themselves to be living in relative affluence. It was easy for them to marry early and to contemplate good-sized families.

But after about two decades an "echo effect" could be discerned. All those postwar babies had grown up and were crowding into the labor market. Their unemployment rates were comparatively high and their incomes low; at least, they seemed low in relation to standards that had been formed in rather affluent households. Young husbands began to think that large families were too expensive, and the result was the lower national birth rate.

Easterlin postulates that this kind of effect will persist into 1975. In the 1965-75 decade the number of persons entering the labor market will be rising steadily: men and women between fifteen and twenty-nine will be increasing from 42 million to 57 million. They will be in a very competitive labor market, will have only narrow educational advantages over their elders in that market, and will have rather expensive notions about the living standards appropriate to young married couples—all of which will work to hold down the birth rate. Easterlin believes that the course of population will probably follow the Census Bureau's "C" projection. This projection assumes that completed family size will decline to an average of 2.8 children, down from the recent 3.2.

We may be several years into the 1970s before there is a conclusive answer to the questions raised by the recent fall-off in births. The women born in the early 1940s, whose intentions are the key to the answer, will still be in their twenties for several more years. It will be 1972 before we can be fairly sure that the women born in 1940 are indeed having smaller families rather than simply having their children at greater intervals; by 1972, these women will be thirty-two and are not likely to have many more children. (Early in 1966, when they were twenty-six, these women had an average of 1.88 children, versus 1.96 at that age for women born in 1936 and 1937.)

If births do take the "C" course, some businessmen are going to be disappointed by the market support they receive from the next rise in births. Purveyors of a wide range of products and services—some obvious examples include diaper services, bicycles, linens, milk, toys, baby furniture, children's clothing, baby food, and soft drinks—must clearly operate in smaller markets than they were anticipating only a few years ago. The number of first births, which are the most critical of all for businessmen in most of these markets, would be around 1,500,000 in 1975 on the "C" projection; on the "B" projection, more widely accepted a few years ago than it is now, the number would be 1,700,000.*

* One startling but largely unreported detail about the recent trend of births in the United States concerns the rise in illegitimacy. While total births have been falling, illegitimate births have been rising—over 300,000 in 1966, which is about 100,000 more than ten years ago. The figure represents about 8 percent of all births—one birth out of twelve. Negro women account for almost two-thirds of reported illegitimate births. (The reporting for them is more complete than for whites, in part because so many Negro births are in public hospitals.) However, the Negro proportion has been declining, and the recent rise in total illegitimate births has been concentrated among whites. Most startling of all, perhaps, is the recent sharp rise in such births to white women who are well past their teen-age years; in the decade after 1955, illegitimate births to white women over twenty-four rose about 50 percent, to 28,000. One likely

Still, the reduced expectations leave a lot of room for market growth. (The number of first births in 1966 was only 1,160,000.) Some growth is just about guaranteed by the number of women who will be coming into the main child-bearing ages. The number of women twenty through thirty-four scarcely increased at all between 1957 and 1963; there were around 17 million of them during those years. But then the totals began rising; they are already up 2 million, will be up another 2 million by 1970, and 4 million more by 1975. The number of first marriages, which totaled 1,400,000 in 1966, is already beginning to rise rapidly, and should hit about 1,800,000, perhaps even a little more, by 1975.

This wave of marriages will be the main force behind a simultaneous boost in the number of households. In 1965 there were 57,300,000 households; in 1975 there will be something like 69 million (the figure is the average of the high and low Census projections). But while the increase for 1965-75 will be 2 million greater than that for 1955-65, the *rate* of rise will continue about the same, at 2 percent a year. The bulk of the increase will come from households headed by young couples (see Fig. 8); these "husband-wife households" will rise about 8 million, to 49,600,000 in 1975 (in the previous decade they were up only 5,300,000). Census projections show little increase, perhaps even a decline, in the number of individuals living alone.

One other critical indicator will also be rising in the years ahead: the rate of population growth in 1970-75 will be up from the recent 1.1 percent to 1.3 percent, even if average family size falls, in line with the "C" projection. The number of children in completed families would have to fall all the way to an average of 2.1 before the population would cease growing altogether.

Much of the discussion about future population growth assumes that the more growth we get, the better off we are.

---

explanation for this trend is the increasing difficulty of arranging for an abortion: hospital rules and police enforcement have both been getting tougher.

Aside from the 300,000-odd women who are not married when they bear children, another 450,000 or so, it appears, become pregnant before they have husbands—and then get married. Studies in the Detroit area, by Ronald Freedman of the University of Michigan, suggest the bride is pregnant in perhaps 20 percent of marriages among whites; the figure is twice as high for Negroes.

Household growth will increase...

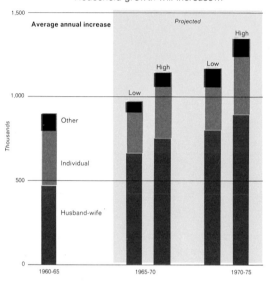

...especially among the young...

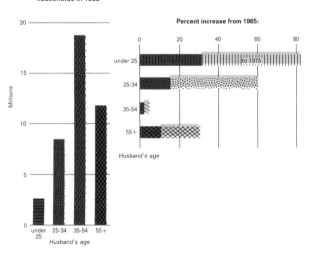

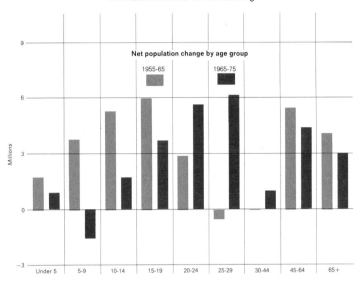

...whose numbers will be soaring.

Net population change by age group

1955-65   1965-75

Millions

9

6

3

0

−3

Under 5   5-9   10-14   15-19   20-24   25-29   30-44   45-64   65+

Fig. 7 (upper left). Households grew by an average of 890,000 a year in 1960-65. The average of the Census Bureau's high and low projections for 1965-70 is 1,050,000 a year, a rise of 18 percent—and another 18 percent rise is expected in the following five years. The gain projected for the period to 1970 has household formation exceeding 1 million annually for the first time since 1947-50. The gain will be concentrated in households that have husbands and wives, as shown in the lower section of the left-hand column. **Fig. 8 (left).** Families in which the husbands were under twenty-five were 6.4 percent of all husband-wife families in 1965, but a tremendous rise in the number of such households has begun. By 1970-75 they will be moving into the next age bracket, and so twenty-five-to-thirty-four-year-old families will also be growing rapidly. In 1965 families with husbands under thirty-five were 27 percent of the total; by 1975 they will constitute about 23 percent. **Fig. 9 (upper right).** In the past decade or so, scores of United States markets were transformed by the special demands of the soaring teen-age population. These affluent youngsters are now moving into their twenties, and are becoming customers for big-ticket items like appliances, furniture, and sporty cars. Young consumers are the most receptive to innovations, and so the years ahead are going to be most auspicious for launching new products for both personal and family use.

In fact, however, there are several areas of American life in which a slowdown will come as something of a relief. Education is certainly one such area. The reduced birth rate has already begun to affect elementary-school enrollments. In the past eight years, attendance has gone up 5,500,000 and Americans have come to take ever-expanding enrollments as part of the order of things. But from 1967 to 1970 the rolls will remain nearly stable; and from 1970 to 1975, on the "C" projection, they will actually decline by 2,500,000. Increases in high-school enrollments will, of course, decline later. Total expenditures on education, which now come to $50 billion including private schools and colleges, may not decline in absolute terms; but they should at least grow less steeply: such expenditures rose by 110 percent in the past eight years, and may go up about half as fast in the next eight. The difference means not only less pressure on state and local budgets, but a new opportunity to improve physical plant and to raise educational quality.

Indeed, the reduced pressure on school systems may make it possible to implement some large education reforms that have come to seem more critical. The idea of getting children, especially slum children, to school earlier, in programs like Head Start, has been spreading. It has been estimated that it would cost a billion dollars a year just to enroll 20 percent of the nation's three- and four-year-olds in school. A lower rate of increase in births would also make it easier to experiment with such new (and expensive) devices as talking typewriters and computers that teach.

A lower population growth rate will not itself affect the labor force for many years; growth of the labor force is, of course, related to the baby crops of previous years. Not all the labor-market effects of the postwar baby boom have been felt yet. The labor force was growing only by 1.1 percent a year in 1956-63, and by 1.8 percent annually in 1964-66, a figure that reflected the rising wave of births after 1946. The over-all growth rate is not likely to rise in the next few years. But in several particular labor markets, where prolonged education is a career prerequisite, the postwar wave hasn't even begun to hit yet. The 1946 generation will not have completed college, graduate school, and military service until the early 1970s—but then, it is predictable, there will be a flood of young engineers, scientists, and executives.

The rapid expansion and increasing youthfulness of the labor force will have several predictable consequences. One will be a somewhat greater availability of capital: husbands and wives in the labor force are savers, in general, while retired families tend to draw down on savings. Another way of viewing the data is to divide the population into "producers" (those in their working years) and "consumers" (those too young to work or old enough to be retired). In 1965, 51 percent of all Americans were between twenty and sixty-five. In the mid-1970s, as more and more young adults pile into the labor force, the proportion will be around 53 percent—and still rising. With the producers increasing more rapidly than the consumers, the population "mix" of the 1970s will be one geared to high living standards.

3

A Slow Getaway
for the Auto Market

ONCE AUTO SALES climb out of the trough they fell into in 1966—so runs a widespread exepectation—they will quickly roar back to the surging pace of 1965. That would be very good for the economy, but it is not likely to happen. In the long run, the market is bound to be strong, for it is as if America were created for the automobile, but over the next few years the growth in new-car sales will be unexciting. After leaping from record to record in the mid-sixties, auto sales—measured by the numbers of new cars sold, not the dollar volume—will show only very moderate growth for the rest of the decade.

On *Fortune*'s estimate the basic auto market in 1970 will run to approximately 9,500,000 new cars (including imports). That's only 200,000 more than the 9,300,000 new cars actually sold in the United States in 1965. But the sluggishness of growth in unit sales will be partly compensated by more spending per car—buyers probably will continue to trade up to more expensive models and load them with more and more accessories. In the early seventies, unit demand will quicken, largely because all those extra cars sold in the mid-sixties will begin to wear out. The market in 1975 will amount to 11,500,000 new cars.

The auto manufacturers themselves are somewhat more cheerful in their estimates. Detroit forecasts average out to a 10-million market in 1970. There may be some wishful thinking in these estimates since the auto makers have been investing heavily, $7 billion in 1964-67, to expand and improve capacity. The manufacturers appear to be a bit more optimistic than *Fortune*'s analysts about some of the factors in the market, and especially about the effects of the postwar baby boom. The auto industry may be overestimating the lift that sales will get as young people born in the baby boom of the later 1940s come into their car-buying years; it seems likely that to a great extent the impact on sales has already been felt.

None of the forecasts, neither the manufacturers' nor *Fortune*'s, apply to the actual, flesh-and-blood years 1970 and 1975; they refer, rather, to the basic markets for those years in a prosperous economy. The auto market is particularly volatile, and, depending upon economic and other conditions, actual sales in any year may be 15 percent or more above or below the projected trend.

While the next few years may be disappointing to Detroit, the long-run prospects still look good. Despite the outcries against the automobile—for fouling the air, killing so many people, and laying waste to city and countryside—the United States remains an automobile-loving society. Sociologists try to explain this phenomenon by telling us that a car removes a man from real life, seals him up in luxury, and responds unquestioningly to his commands. There is a more prosaic explanation: more and more Americans can and want to move about, and increasingly the automobile is the most convenient way of doing so. The continuing dispersion and suburbanization of American life occur only because the automobile makes them possible. More income, more education, more working wives, and even "the pill" all favor the car—the pill because it postpones children in the young family and so leaves more money to buy a car and more time to go places in it.

Fortune's analysis of future auto sales begins with a pair of reliable facts: there are now over 70 million cars on the road, and in time they will all have to be scrapped and replaced. Some economists argue that to try to divine the new-car market from the scrappage rate is like speculating on a woman's new wardrobe by picking through what she has given away to the Salvation Army. The lady buys new rags and throws away old rags, but she doesn't necessarily do the one as a result of doing the other. In the auto market, however, there is a connection between scrappage of old and purchase of new. The driver who gives up on an old heap ready for scrapping does not have a lot of other cars hanging in his wardrobe, and unless he stops driving he needs another car. That man rarely buys a new one, but the former owner of the used car he buys needs to get another car; eventually, in the chain of trades, someone does buy a new car. Scrappage creates a basic replacement need that is the foundation of the new-car market. Even if there were no increase at all from year to year in the total number of cars in use, the auto industry would still have to produce several million new cars each year to replace the old cars scrapped.

A car wears out, on the average, ten years and 100,000 miles after it is built. Since most of the cars that will be scrapped in the next ten years are already on the road, it is possible to construct scrappage rate trends for the period. Because sales were drab in the late fifties and the first two years of the sixties, the basic scrappage rate, which is now 6 million, will increase slowly over the next few years to 6,700,000 in 1970. But later on, because the mid-sixties were big new-car years, scrappage will increase more quickly, to 8,200,000 in 1975. These are trend figures. Like new-car sales, scrappage is volatile—in bad years people keep their old cars running a little longer. But the below-trend and above-trend years average out.

Replacement demand has accounted for 62 to 76 percent of total demand during the last decade. The remainder, the growth component of the market, can be traced to (1) households acquiring a car for the first time, (2) car-owning households buying additional cars, and (3) business and government purchases.

Prior to World War II the market grew mainly because established households were buying their first cars. Now nearly 80 percent of all households own at least one car, and by reason of age, ill health, poverty, or exceptional location (such as crowded, cramped Manhattan), a great many of the other 20 percent will remain carless. Accordingly, growth in the number of car-owning households largely depends upon formations of new households. These averaged about one million a year during the sixties, but the rate is rising, and in 1970, by Census Bureau estimate, 1,100,000 households will be formed. Putting together purchases by new households and the trickle of first-time purchases by established households, *Fortune* projects a combined first-car growth factor of 1,200,000 new cars in 1970 and 1,350,-000 in 1975.

Purchases of second cars will add about as many units to the market as purchases of first cars. Since 1960 the number of families with two or more cars has risen from nearly 10,000,000 to nearly 14,800,000. One household in four now owns two or more cars. There are continuing reasons for purchases of second cars: the move to the suburbs, higher incomes, working wives who need cars to get to their jobs. Since 1960, according to figures derived from Department of Commerce and private sample surveys, second-car purchases have probably added an average of almost 900,000 cars to the market every year. The growth has been steady, and the reasons for it are still in effect, so projections of two-car growth are pretty solid. Two-car demand should add 1,100,000 autos to the market in 1970 and 1,400,000 in 1975.

Apart from scrappage and first- and second-car purchases by households, there are additional components of sales that are hard to pin down: purchases of third and fourth cars by households and purchases by business and government. Surprisingly, statistics on these categories are sketchy, and it is difficult to sort them out with precision. Accordingly, they are grouped together as "other" growth in Fig. 10.

This "other" category is a residual, derived by subtracting the known factors from total cars on the road. A further complication is that this residual has behaved erratically. It jumped from an average of 230,000 a year in 1960-63 to 850,000 a year in 1964-66. Since government and business purchases grow at a moderate rate (even with the growth of rental fleets), there must be another explanation for this explosion. It has to be an effect of the postwar baby boom. Children born in 1946 became eighteen in 1964. A small army of youngsters has been influencing the auto market by pestering parents for a car. The youngsters may have bought cars of their own, or had cars passed on to them, or caused cars to be bought. One way or another, they contributed to the boom in auto sales in the mid-sixties, partly by adding to the numbers of third or fourth cars purchased by households. Some of these purchases apparently escaped being counted in surveys of household car ownership.

In other words, the postwar baby boom has already hit the auto market. Moreover, the growth rate of the population group aged eighteen to twenty-one will slow down in the next few years. The growth of this age group averaged only 200,000 annually during the last half of the fifties, increased to 400,000 annually in the early sixties, and then leaped to a current average of 700,000. The year-to-year increase will ease off after 1968 and settle down to a little over 200,000 in the seventies. Therefore *Fortune* estimates that third- and fourth-car purchases by households will be a minor *growth* factor, around 250,000 in 1970 and the same in 1975. Business and government purchases will add a small, steady increment to the market, 250,000 in 1970 and 300,000 in 1975. Adding up the two, *Fortune* projects a growth of 500,000 cars in 1970 and 550,000 in 1975 in the residual or "other" growth category.

The market projections can be summarized as follows:

	1970	1975
	(in millions)	
Replacements (scrappage)	6.7	8.2
Growth factors		
First-car households	1.2	1.35
Second-car households	1.1	1.4
Other	.5	.55
Total new-car sales	9.5	11.5

Actual sales will, of course, swing above and below the trend line from year to year because of temporary factors,

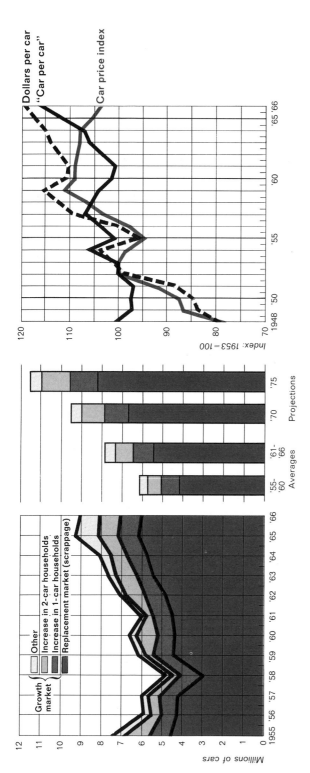

The Anatomy of Auto Sales

Fig. 10. The market for new automobiles (chart at left) is the sum of "replacement" (for cars scrapped) and "growth." The "other" category shown on the chart combines third- and fourth-car purchases and business and government purchases. Over the next several years, dollar volume should grow faster than unit sales. The average expenditure per new car (broken line, chart at right) increased during the sixties, but that happened because of "trading up" to higher-priced models and "plussing up" with extras. The Bureau of Labor Statistics retail index of basic new-car prices, which adjusts for year-to-year changes in cars, has been declining—consumers have been getting more car per dollar while spending more dollars per car. So "car per car" (black line), the average real value of the new cars purchased, has been rising steeply.

including the appeal, or lack of it, of the latest models. The auto companies, through their research departments and consultants, are trying to tune themselves more finely than ever to what the public wants. There is always pressure to innovate, but there is also a compulsion to stick with success. "The industry," Ford Vice-President Donald Frey has said, "tends to work itself into a box, into patterns indicated by temporary public acceptance. The rewards for breaking out of the box are increasing."

The penalties for making the wrong break are also increasing, because there are so many models to choose from. The Mustang is the best recent example of the right break. Consumer reaction was tested in advance perhaps more thoroughly than for any other car in history. Even so, Ford greatly underestimated the market. It was to be the young person's car. It turned out to be everyone's car. There is still a lot of luck in launching styles.

Auto makers appear now to be working themselves into a box rather than trying their luck again. They assert that no radical departures in style are imminent, and that any significant innovations, such as electric cars or turbine cars, are still at least five years away. The trend, then, is toward more of what is now on the road.

For the next few years, until it becomes a bore, "sportiness," the Mustang theme, will dominate styling. The "sporty" car is not merely a fad. There has been a major change in taste. So long as there was one car in the family, it tended to be a practical sedan or station wagon. Now that there are more cars in relation to people, the individual can pick a car more specifically suited to his needs, and the family can pick several cars suited to several needs. So the old four-door sedan and the station wagon have gone into a relative decline, and the more amusing hardtops and "sporty" cars have been the big gainers.

To meet the diversification of tastes, automobile models have proliferated. For the Big Three, proliferation has meant the introduction of waves of new cars. Counting different nameplates and types, General Motors in 1967 made 181 kinds of cars, compared to 88 in 1957. Detroit has failed to proliferate only in the low-priced zone. This is one reason for the popularity of the imports, which, with the forceful addition of Japanese competitors, rose from 4.8 percent of the market in 1962 to 7.3 percent in 1966. Imports might capture more of the market unless the Big Three stop scorning the low-priced range.

Detroit's proliferation is often no more than skin deep. While the Mustang may look sporty, it shares a lot of innards with the modest Falcon. But proliferation has meant expensive tooling, and only because sales were so high in the middle sixties could the auto makers afford it. Now the number of models offered is nearing a plateau. So in the next few years auto sales will miss the extra boost they got in recent years from the burst of diversity.

The sporty look, the low car with the long hood, is influencing the styles of all cars. Even Cadillac, which has "no sports content," as one auto maker puts it, has produced a front-wheel-drive Eldorado with decidedly sporty lines. Victor Raviolo, group vice-president at American Motors, has predicted that within a decade, instead of the separate sporty and standard lines that exist now, each standard car will have its sporty version. In between will be the hardtops, which will become more like sporty cars, perhaps lower and with a more rakish windshield. Another style characteristic that has taken hold is the "hop-up in the rear quarter," which gives GM cars their Coke-bottle shape and is spreading to other makes.

There is a certain amount of hokum in the sporty cars. They are made to look athletic but they don't have the performance that the looks imply, at least not without major modifications. They are not sports cars. There is also hokum in the "personalized" car, a term conveying the result of the proliferation of models, options, and accessories. "Personalization" puts a custom icing on a mass-produced car. It takes the plain Plymouth Belvedere, honest transportation ($2,412 f.o.b. Detroit), and turns it into the Belvedere GTX, a "supercar" equipped with special suspension, brakes, and exhaust, even a "pit-stop gas filler" and hood scoops, and powered by the "awesome Hemi" with its "426 cubes" ($3,930).

Hokum or not, "personalization" is one of the trends that have made sales of options and of accessories very strong. At Chrysler, although unit sales were down more than 15 percent in the first quarter of 1967, the dollar volume of factory-installed accessory sales was up over 1966. Air-conditioning has caught on so well that upwards of 20,000 air-conditioned Volkswagens a year are sold in the United States. When Lincoln receives an order for a Continental without air-conditioning, the district office automatically questions the order. In 1957, 3.4 percent of the new cars sold were equipped with air-conditioners. In 1966 the percentage was up to 29.3. At about $400 per car, this accessory alone was enough to add almost $1 billion to car sales in 1967. That is the dollar equivalent of over 300,000 cars. The proportion of air-conditioners shows signs of going right on up to the level of, say, power steering (two out of every three new cars).

Fancier gadgets and fancier cars are probably Detroit's best bet for increasing dollar sales in the near future. Unit demand, by the *Fortune* projections, will increase at a slower rate in the next three years than the potential 4-percent annual increase in real personal income. Yet there is no reason to suppose that Americans will not continue to spend around 4.5 percent of their growing disposable income for cars, as they have been doing. In other words, consumers will have more to spend per car. This is already evident in the growth in option and accessory sales, which will continue to expand.

It is also evident in trading up toward the "top of the line." Dr. George Katona, director of economic research at the Survey Research Center at Ann Arbor, Michigan, takes periodic surveys to follow trends of auto sales by price categories. The greatest sales increase between 1961 and 1965 occurred in cars priced at $3,500 and more, and the next greatest in cars between $3,000 and $3,499. The average expenditure per new United States-made car, in constant dollars, increased by 6.1 percent from 1961 to 1964, then by 8.3 percent from 1964 to 1966. In short, the trend has accelerated.

The suction upward, caused by disposable income increasing at a faster rate than unit sales, will encourage Detroit to go on selling more "car per car"—that is, to make cars bigger, more powerful, more luxurious, more loaded with extras. The trend to additional inches and horsepower hints faintly at a repetition of the disaster of the fifties, when Detroit added so much car per car that the customers finally revolted against the "insolent chariots."

The growth in disposable income will also encourage Detroit to raise prices. In the last ten years auto prices have been remarkably stable. The Bureau of Labor Statistics figures that new-car prices have actually been declining since 1961 despite the rising average expenditure per car (see Fig. 10). This statistical surprise involves, says one auto maker, the help of "some honest weaseling." The BLS retail index of basic new-car prices is adjusted for changes in the quality of the autos measured. For instance, when heaters began to be standard instead of optional equipment, this worked to reduce the index because there was not a corresponding price increase. The trimming of the federal excise tax, moreover, has helped keep the BLS index down. In any case, since the over-all consumer price index has risen by 8.5 percent since 1961, the auto has enjoyed a splendid advantage in relative price, which was one reason for strong auto sales in the mid-sixties.

Usually auto makers are very discreet in talking about price increases, but now they are saying frankly they think factory prices will go up in the next few years. Pressures are accumulating. Wages increased 12 percent in the period 1963-66, and the new three-year contracts with the United Auto Workers call for a raise, in pay and fringe benefits, of around 7 percent a year—which adds about 2 percent to the cost of producing a car. Another cost pusher is the new federal safety law. The safety regulations that went into effect for 1968 models have added $50 to $60 worth of equipment to a car. The anti-pollution standards required in California have also become mandatory for new cars throughout the United States with the 1968 models, and that has added anywhere up to another $50.

Detroit is not sure what the price increases attributable to anti-pollution and safety devices will do to the market. Unlike the enticing optional extras, these devices constitute an additional expense imposed upon, rather than chosen by, the consumer. If auto sales obeyed what economists call "unit elasticity," a 1-percent increase in price should cause a 1-percent decrease in sales. Looking at all the market factors, GM seems to be less pessimistic than Ford about what the actual effects will be.

There is also disagreement as to whether the talk about safety has had any impact on sales. In his surveys of consumers, Dr. Katona finds very little concern about the safety of the car. (Nor are drivers overly bothered by heavy traffic or repair bills, he says; what they really complain about is the shortage of downtown parking space.) But Sindlinger & Company, the market-research firm, attributes the depth of last year's decline in auto sales to "confusion" over safety. Certainly Corvair has almost died in reaction to Ralph Nader's bill of complaints against earlier models. If there is a concern about safety, it will probably be only a short-term check on the market; sooner or later those who are postponing purchases while waiting for safer cars will decide to buy. By 1970, according to Dr. William Haddon, federal traffic-safety administrator, new safety equipment will make it "almost impossible to kill yourself at suburban or commuting speed" (i.e., about 45 mph). If cars become clearly safer, that would tend to hasten scrappage of older cars, which lack the safety devices.

Beyond the direct effects that the costs of safety and pollution equipment may have on sales, there is a question whether growing social hostility will begin to cool the basic American passion for the automobile. Social critics have made us aware of the environmental damage done by the automobile, and legislatures have passed, or talked about passing, laws in defense of man against the auto. At a conference on pollution in December 1966, Secretary of Health, Education, and Welfare Gardner said that "perhaps we also need to find other ways of moving people around" and that "the day may come when we may have to trade convenience for survival."

For all the furor, there is no evidence that Americans would give up the convenience unless they could neither move nor breathe for the traffic and fumes. George Brown, Ford's director of marketing research, has happily said: "People find the over-all benefits of personal transport so great, they will own and operate a car under almost any circumstances."

Despite the stereotype nightmare of city centers paved with immobilized cars, the convenience of a car is really increasing. Intercity travel by car, which already accounts for more than 90 percent of all intercity travel, has been getting faster and therefore more popular. The drive between New York and Chicago took twenty-five hours in the early 1950s and now can be completed (legally) in seventeen hours. According to a study of city transport and parking done for the

Automobile Manufacturers Association by Wilbur Smith & Associates, transportation engineering consultant, auto travel within metropolitan areas has noticeably quickened. In the Los Angeles area the average peak-hour speed on the freeways increased from 24 mph in 1957 to 32.5 mph in 1965.

Wilbur Smith has predicted a moderate increase in public-transit travel, confined mainly to the very biggest cities (four-fifths of all rapid-transit passengers in the United States are in New York); but autos will carry the bulk of the big increase expected in metropolitan-area transportation. For all its concern with other forms of transportation, the federal government will probably increase its highway spending above the present annual level of $4.3 billion. Road planners in Washington are turning their attention to city freeways and parking. New York State's $2.5-billion bond authorization for transportation includes more money for highways than for mass transit. "We are going to need all the transit we can get," Chrysler Chairman Lynn Townsend has said. "The risk is that people will think that mass transit is a substitute for the auto. It isn't."

The automobile is being attacked as the enemy of the city's soul. If the battle between auto and city were just beginning, this attack might be a serious challenge. But the growth in downtown auto traffic will be slow because homes and jobs—and therefore traffic—are moving to the suburbs. The auto is turning elsewhere for new asphalt pastures.

It is the growing suburbs that guarantee the strength of the auto market. A Rand Corporation study has estimated there will be a 16-percent shift of metropolitan-area populations from center to suburb between 1965 and 1975, and a 20-percent shift in employment from center to suburb. By 1975, says Rand, 72 percent of the people and 56 percent of the jobs in metropolitan areas will be in the suburbs. Even now, in New York's Westchester County, it sometimes seems that rush-hour traffic is going the wrong way.

Suburbanization will continue to create more diffused traffic patterns. Large rush-hour movements of people to downtown employment suit mass transit, but highly individual movements among suburbs require automobiles. As the United States prospers, Americans consume more space and therefore require more transport. Transportation needs in general are expanding, but the auto market is not simply growing along with the other types of surface transportation —it is growing faster.

Still, there must be, somewhere out there, a practical limit to the number of cars Americans are willing to own. The Federal Bureau of Public Roads sees a possible limiting factor in the ratio of licensed drivers to total autos on the road. This ratio has narrowed from an estimated 1.63 in 1949 to 1.42 in 1957 and 1.3 in 1967. The auto population curve has begun to bump against the human population curve and level off. There is, of course, no demographic law that says the vehicle curve cannot push right through the human curve. If a family really wants to own a fleet of cars, one to suit each mood of each member, then maybe it will; but each extra car is less worth having.

AMC's Raviolo is one auto-industry executive who sees the beginning of saturation. A family's first car, he says, is a "necessity," and the second a "great convenience," but the third is a "plaything." The first car has little competition for the consumer's dollar, but by the third car the consumer's choice might be whether to buy a sports car or a boat or a trip around the world.

The possibility of saturation, however, cannot now be considered a serious threat to the auto market, and neither can the issues of pollution and safety. The auto makers will be subjected to more of what Henry Ford II has chosen to call "harassment," that is, regulation, but there is no evidence that the problems created by the auto are going to be solved by a substitute. Other kinds of transit and other kinds of vehicles can only supplement the auto. Even if the electric car came into wide use, it would probably be an increment to the market for cars with internal-combustion engines— and anyhow would be produced by the auto makers. Moreover, the stake in the internal-combustion engine is so huge that huge resources can be used to save it. Automobile pollution is more likely to be reduced through improvements in the internal-combustion engine and in fuels than through general use of a different kind of car or engine.

The automobile can survive the problems it has created. The real strength of the auto market is that the ways of life of American society, having been shaped by the auto, must have the auto.

4

That Coming Boom in Housing

WITH SOME of the natural inevitability of tides or seasons, a housing boom is coming. Children born during the postwar baby boom have begun entering their twenties, and in the years just ahead they will, in swelling numbers, be forming their own households. That much about the prospects for housing has been widely foreseen for quite some years now. No great effort of mind, after all, is involved in grasping that a person born in 1946 comes of age in 1967. It has been too casually assumed, however, that a great increase in demand for housing units would automatically translate into a commensurately large increase in the dollar volume of new housing. Maybe it will. But how big a boom it will be in its economic effects will largely depend upon the mix—the kinds and sizes of the new units—and the mix, in turn, will depend upon some rather inscrutable factors, including the performance of the housing industry itself.

In any event, we are going to be seeing a lot of new housing units built over the next several years. On *Fortune*'s estimates, total housing starts should average 2 million a year in the first half of the seventies, and the rate should get up close to that by the end of the sixties. These are impressive numbers, not only compared to 1966's 1,250,000 total, pinched by tight money, but also compared to the 1,450,000 average of the past ten years. Even over the ten years before *that*, taking in the period when construction was making up for the big housing deficit left by the depression and the war, total starts averaged only a bit more than 1,500,000 a year.

As Fig. 11 indicates, housing has been in a general downtrend, relative to gross national product, since 1950. Housing missed the boom of the past several years. Looking back on those years, G. T. Bogard, head of General Electric's division involved in developing "new cities," observed that housing is "the only major industry failing to participate in the greatest economic boom the world has ever known." Within a year or two, however, the situation may be just the reverse, with housing construction outpacing the economy as a whole.

The prospect of a major upturn in housing would be important for the economy at any time, but the coming upturn takes on special importance in view of the possibility that some other forces of demand may be a bit sluggish over the next several years. As was pointed out in the first chapter, the 1962-66 boom was powered mainly by the surging expansion of capital investment, plus extraordinarily strong demand for consumer goods (and, of course, the Vietnam war); in the period 1967-71, capital spending will certainly be expanding at a less rapid pace, and consumer spending for goods may be less exuberant. Housing will be able to take up some of the slack—perhaps a lot of it. And construction of a great many new housing units, of course, implies fortified demand for furniture, household equipment, and utilities, as well as for public facilities.

The gaudy-looking estimate of 2 million housing starts a year in the first half of the seventies, moreover, significantly understates the total housing market, for it leaves out that anomalous housing category, mobile homes. Not counted as housing in the federal government's economic statistics, mobile homes are generally overlooked or underestimated in analyses of the housing market, but since large numbers of people live in them, they obviously constitute part of the housing supply. In recent years, indeed, mobile homes have accounted for an enlarging share of the total housing market, and that trend will probably continue. Shipments ran well above 200,000 a year in 1965 and 1966, nearly double the level of the late fifties. On *Fortune*'s estimates, shipments should average at least 250,000 a year over the rest of the decade and 350,000 or more in the early seventies.

Some observers have argued that the mobile-home boom can't last. They point to, among other things, the decreasing availability of mobile-home parks, discrimination in zoning, omission of mobiles in community planning. But the industry has a powerful and probably decisive advantage going for it: mobile homes cost a lot less than conventional one-family housing. The average retail price of mobiles in 1966, according to the trade association, came to $5,700 furnished. Conventional builders cannot come close to matching that. To widen the market, the mobile-home industry has developed larger, more houselike units, delivered in two sections that are fastened together at the site. Some makers are convinced that "sectionalized" units attached to permanent foundations will supply a growing share of the market for $8,000-to-$12,000 housing, a market left wide open by the housing industry. Newton Glekel, president of Divco-Wayne Corporation, a major producer of mobiles, has said: "When you think of mobile homes, think of low-cost housing."

Though a boom in housing construction is doubtless on the way, it will, paradoxically, begin rather drably. Total starts will increase slowly, for it will take time for the numbing effects of the recent mortgage crunch to wear off. The Vietnam war, moreover, is holding back family formations. The housing boom, in short, will be getting off to a late start.

Once it gets going, however, it will run all the faster for having started late. Even without the lags of 1966 and 1967, the normal potential market in 1968-69 would average better than 1,700,000 starts a year. But the gap between potential demand and actual construction in 1966 reduced the vacancy rate to the lowest level in quite a few years; a backlog of demand has been building up. By 1969, as a result, housing starts might climb all the way to the 2-million level projected for the first half of the seventies.

Whether housing construction actually gets that high in 1969, or averages that high in the first half of the next decade, will to a great extent depend upon factors other than potential demand. It is by no means certain that the housing industry will be capable of building 2 million units a year, or that enough mortgage money will be available to finance 2 million a year. What is certain is that the potential markets will be there.

Any estimate of potential housing demand in the late sixties and early seventies begins with projections of household formations. What counts here, of course, is *net* formations. Over any span of time, new households are formed and existing households are dissolved, by deaths or other eventualities, and it is the net change that affects aggregate demand for housing units. *Fortune*'s estimates of net household formations are based upon revised projections recently issued by the Bureau of the Census. The bureau provides "high" and "low" alternatives, which are about 200,000 apart, and *Fortune* simply averaged these, since it seems reasonable to suppose that the actualities will fall between.

During the first half of the 1960s the number of households increased by an average of just under 900,000 a year. The yearly increase will average 1,050,000 during the second half of the sixties and 1,250,000 during the first half of the seventies. In other words, the year-to-year increase in the total number of households will run more than 350,000 higher during the early seventies than during the early sixties. This demographic picture is the principal basis for the expectation of a boom in demand for housing.

But this is not the only one. A hefty impetus to housing construction will come from the growing demand for second homes. These can take any of a great variety of forms, but whatever the form, be it house, shack, or apartment, it will lie at some distance from a city and be occupied only part of the time. Several powerful factors will be working to expand this market—increasing leisure, the growing popularity of outdoor recreation, rising levels of discretionary income, expanding road networks providing access by car to more and more potential sites for second homes, and the psychological need to escape from increasingly congested metropolitan areas.

Nobody knows with any certainty how many second homes

The Long Downtrend

Fig. 11. The great postwar surge in housing peaked back in 1950, and since then the relative importance of housing in the economy has trended downward. The chart shows total expenditures for new residential structures as a percentage of gross national product. Each successive peak from 1950 on is lower than the one before, and so is each successive trough. In 1965, before the tight money of 1966 curtailed housing, the percentage had already reached its lowest point since 1946. In 1966, of course, the percentage fell sharply. It is bound to rise from this depth, but even during the coming upturn it seems unlikely that housing's share of GNP can get as high as the 1950 peak.

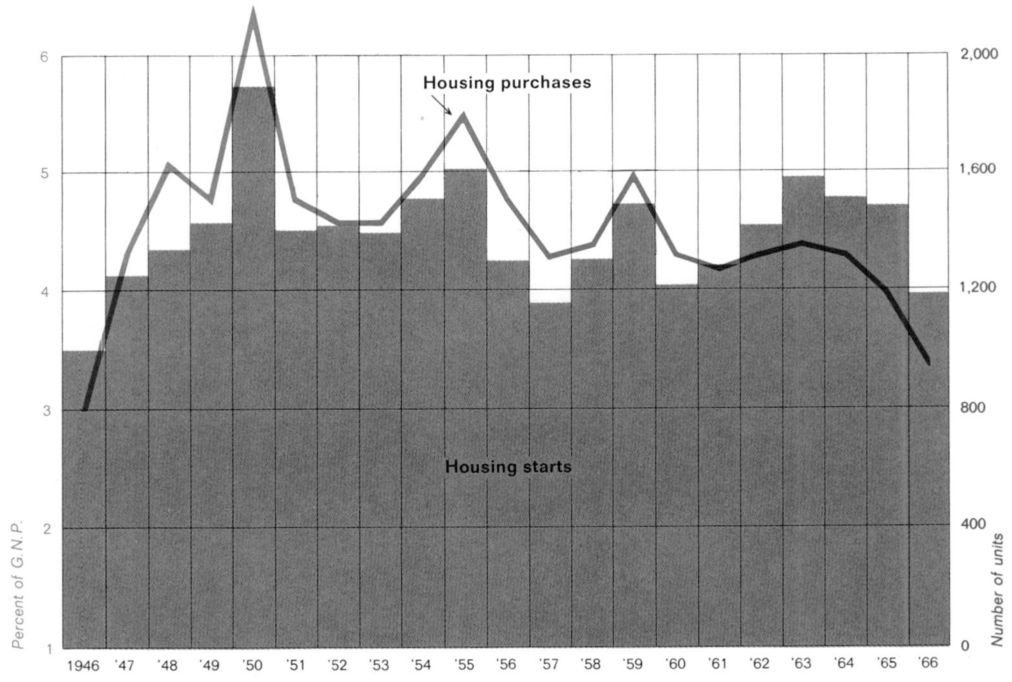

have been built in recent years. Bureau of the Census data imply an increase of about 50,000 second homes a year during the early sixties, and a current total stock of about 2,300,000 units, but there are good reasons to question these figures. Various other surveys of second-home ownership have come up with substantially higher numbers. Weyerhaeuser Company, using data collected in a large-scale survey of telephone households in 1965, concluded that nearly 3 million families owned second homes, and this finding omitted vacation units owned as income-producing property and rented out to various tenants over the course of a year. Moreover, discrepancies within Census data covering the fifties suggest that census-takers may have mistakenly counted significant numbers of second homes as year-round homes.

On *Fortune*'s estimate, the number of second homes increased by at least 100,000 a year in the early sixties. Starting from this higher base, *Fortune* projects a potential second-home market of 150,000 units a year in the later sixties and 200,000 a year in the early seventies. In addition, the number of mobile homes used as vacation houses will be increasing by about 50,000 a year.

The total market for new housing units over any period of time can be looked upon as the sum of four components. Two of these we have already considered: the increases in households and second homes. The third component is the increase, if any, in the number of vacant housing units (other than second homes). Finally, you have to take into account "removals," that is, housing units demolished, destroyed by fire, or otherwise removed from the housing stock. Even if households, second homes, and vacancies remained constant over a period of time, there would still be a need for new housing units to make up for removals (somewhat as new automobiles are required to make up for those that are scrapped).

In working out its estimates of total housing demand in the late sixties and early seventies, *Fortune* assumed that both the vacancy rate and the removal rate—as a percentage of the total housing stock—would remain constant. But, of course, if the vacancy *rate* remains constant over a span of years, the number of vacant units nevertheless increases as the total housing stock expands; so, too, with removals.

The removal rate used in *Fortune*'s calculations of future housing demand is 0.6 percent. This was just about the average rate for the fifties. On this basis, removals would increase from about 350,000 a year in the early sixties to an average of 400,000 in the second half of the sixties and 450,000 in the first half of the seventies.

Some housing experts project much bigger figures for scrappage in the years ahead. The National Association of Home Builders, for example, works with a removal rate of approximately 1 percent in estimating housing demand for the late sixties and early seventies. The choice of a higher rate traces in part to a sharp statistical rise in removals during the last few years of the fifties. But *Fortune*'s analysis of housing data for the early sixties confirms the 0.6 figure, and indicates that the rise in the late fifties was an aberration. As a matter of statistical procedure, moreover, use of the longer-term average for the entire decade of the fifties reduces the probable error and provides a more stable, and hence more reliable, figure to work with.

A dance on a statistical pinhead? Far from it: the difference between *Fortune*'s scrappage rate of 0.6 percent and the NAHB's 1 percent is equivalent to some 300,000 housing units a year in the projections of the housing market of the early seventies. It should be remembered that, high as they may seem by the standards of the recent past, *Fortune*'s projections of housing demand are less exuberant than those of the NAHB and some other organizations in the housing field.

So far we have looked at the potential housing market exclusively in terms of numbers of units. But the economic heft of the coming housing boom will depend, of course, upon the dollar totals involved rather than the numbers of units. Any attempt to forecast the magnitude of the boom in terms of dollars would involve excessively arbitrary assumptions relating to the future housing mix. The mix will be affected both by what people want in the way of housing and by what the housing industry provides, and there are impenetrable uncertainties on both sides. But it is possible to discern some influences that will be operating, some limitations and potentialities.

For one thing, it is clear that a big percentage of the housing units built over the next several years are going to be apartments. The age structure of the population points to booming demand for apartments. During the late sixties and the early seventies the number of younger households (where the head is under thirty-five) will be rising rapidly. In contrast, the number of households headed by persons in their middle years, thirty-five through fifty-four, will hardly increase at all. The latter group, of course, includes a far higher proportion of home-owners, and accounts for a lopsidedly greater percentage of the purchases of higher-priced houses.

Some experts forecast a fifty-fifty split between houses and apartments in housing starts over the next several years, but the trend to apartments probably won't go quite that far that fast. Until now, apartment living as a way of life has been concentrated in New York, Los Angeles, and a few other big cities. If apartments were to account for as much as 50 percent of all housing starts over the late sixties and early seventies, that would mean a large-scale diffusion of apartments throughout the United States. Enormous numbers of families whose age-and-income counterparts in the fifties lived in houses would have to choose to live in apartments. It may be a bit unrealistic to expect preferences in styles of life to shift that rapidly. But in view of the age structure of the population, it is clear that over the next several years the apartment share in total housing starts will at least match the one-third level of recent years. Even that kind of share for apartments will bring an extensive spread of apartment living.

With apartments accounting for at least one-third of the new starts, the total dollar value of new housing in the years ahead, and therefore the contribution of housing to the gross national product, will be a lot smaller than if the market for one-family houses exploded. From what they have seen going up around them, residents of Manhattan's East Side or Chicago's lakefront or San Francisco's Nob Hill might suppose that most of the new apartments built in recent years have been luxury units in high-rise buildings. But in fact most of them have been smallish units in garden developments. Nearly four-fifths of all apartment starts in 1965 were contained in buildings of three stories or less. In recent years the average construction cost of apartments has run to not much more than half the average for one-family houses. No wonder, then, that, measured in constant dollars,

The Changing Mix

Fig. 12. During the early sixties, houses accounted for a sharply declining share of total new housing units. The number of houses built each year ran far below the average of the fifties. In apartments, by contrast, a major uptrend began in 1961, and the number of apartments started doubled within a few years. Meanwhile mobile homes were also booming. Last year mobile-home shipments held up well, but house and apartment starts dropped sharply. For apartments, it was the first important decline in a decade and a half. The figures do not include public housing (mostly apartments) or farm units (a relatively tiny segment of the total housing market).

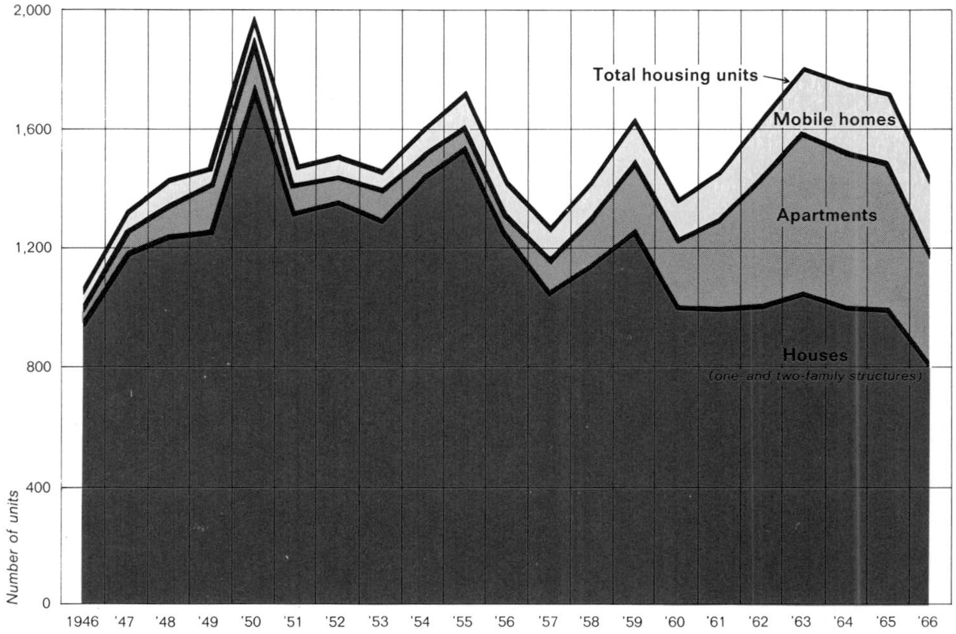

Chart labels:
Total housing units
Mobile homes
Apartments
Houses *(one- and two-family structures)*

Y-axis: Number of units — 0, 400, 800, 1,200, 1,600, 2,000

X-axis: 1946, '47, '48, '49, '50, '51, '52, '53, '54, '55, '56, '57, '58, '59, '60, '61, '62, '63, '64, '65, '66

the average construction cost of new housing units shrank from the late fifties to the middle sixties—by 7 percent, on *Fortune*'s estimate.

The concentration of apartment starts in moderate-rent garden developments will probably continue to prevail in the years ahead. Various considerations, moreover, suggest that much of the demand for new one-family houses will fall toward the lower end of the price range. The new second homes, of course, will be mostly compact and inexpensive units. And the prospect of virtually no change in the total number of households headed by persons in their middle years points to restrained demand for higher-priced houses. All this suggests that the economy may get much less lift from housing than those expansive projections of household formations have led some observers to assume.

On the other hand, an assessment of the housing market in the early seventies has to take into account what can be called the "income potential," the latent housing market created by rising levels of disposable income. So far, the sixties have witnessed a widening discrepancy between rising incomes and laggard housing. The real value of the total housing stock has been increasing at a slower rate than real income. The gap between the two growth rates has amounted to 1 or 2 percent a year.

According to an often cited yardstick, a family can, conservatively, afford to buy a house costing twice annual income before taxes. By that yardstick, families have not been keeping up with the Joneses of earlier years. The total number of houses with a market value of $20,000 or more has been increasing much less rapidly than the number of families with incomes of $10,000 or more. Over the period 1960-66, by *Fortune*'s calculations, fewer than two million houses priced at $20,000 or more were built in the entire United States. That represents about one-quarter of the number of families that moved up into the $10,000-or-better income category over the same span of time. Some of these families moved into higher-rent apartments, others increased the value of their houses through additions and alterations, and still others bought a second home instead of a bigger or better year-round house. But a great many families with rising incomes have simply not readjusted their housing standards upward commensurately with their new affluence.

Some lag between income levels and housing standards is normal and inevitable. Various human considerations may induce a family to stay put long after its income, by the two-to-one ratio, outgrows its house—attachments to the community, the neighborhood, a church, a school, a garden, or the house itself. For a family that has formed such attachments, it may not seem worth while to move to a more expensive house, with all the bother and frictional expense involved in moving, unless it is a *much* better house. Whether a family whose income has gone up buys a more expensive house, moreover, depends in part upon how readily it can sell the less expensive house. In the early sixties the number of new households formed each year was somewhat smaller than in the late fifties, and that presumably helped restrain demand for lower-priced houses. If the demand had been stronger, more families might have moved to higher-priced houses.

But these considerations cannot fully account for the widening discrepancy between incomes and housing standards that has shown up in the sixties. Other forces must have been at work to bring about the declines illustrated in Figs. 11 and 12: the general downtrend in housing as a share of gross national product, and the relative sag of the one-family house. In view of the traditional importance that Americans have attached to housing and home-ownership, that shrinkage in the average real construction cost of new housing units during a period of rapidly rising real income per family is a stunning social-economic phenomenon.

The future housing mix, and the total dollar volume of new housing construction, will largely depend upon the extent to which altered circumstances can divert a larger share of income into purchases of housing. A widespread upgrading of housing standards, displacing a portion of total demand for new units from garden apartments to houses and from lower-priced houses to higher-priced houses, could add several billion dollars a year to the money volume of new housing construction, even if it added nothing to the number of new units started.

That will not happen, however, unless much else changes. Purchases of new housing have declined relative to income in part because the one-family house has offered the purchaser less and less for his money. For some years now, various factors have operated to increase the cost of home-ownership relative to the benefits.

One of these factors is the relentless climb of land prices in and near metropolitan areas. Fairly typical has been the postwar rise in land prices in the Philadelphia area, the subject of a study recently completed by Professor Grace Milgram of the University of Pennsylvania under a grant from the federal Department of Housing and Urban Development. According to her research, covering a 25,000-acre segment of the metropolitan area, prices rose from an average of $1,030 an acre in 1945 to $13,300 in 1962.

With land prices rising steeply, land has accounted for an ever larger share of what the purchasers pay for new houses. In 1952, according to FHA data, land cost represented 10 percent, on average, of the total price of new single-family houses with mortgages insured by the FHA. By 1957 the land-cost share had risen to 15 percent. In 1966 it averaged 20 percent. And the FHA figures, covering an unrepresentative sample of all one-family houses, probably understate the extent of the rise in land prices. For the period 1963-66, FHA figures showed lot prices going up about 7.5 percent a year, but home-builders reported a very much steeper rate of rise.

The cumulative effects of rocketing land prices help explain both the long downtrend in housing as a share of GNP and the relative decline of the one-family house. In the reckoning of GNP, the land costs of new housing are not counted at all—economists look upon transfers of land as mere exchanges of property, generating no economic product. As land prices rise, accordingly, a given volume of new-house sales represents a smaller and smaller contribution to GNP. And rising land costs, of course, favor apartments as against one-family houses.

Experts in these matters pretty much agree that population growth over the next ten years will concentrate in or near the existing major metropolitan areas, and this prospect points to a continuing climb in building-lot costs. Builders can hold down on land cost per house by building farther and farther beyond city limits, but the growth of mass markets for year-round houses out beyond commuting range will depend upon the extent to which employment moves out.

The dispersion of employment beyond present metropolitan areas may eventually sustain new towns, and even new cities, not tied to presently existing cities by umbilical links of daily commuter traffic. In new towns or cities, built on relatively cheap land, builders would be able to offer more house for the money. But if new cities have any great future, it is a future beyond the time horizon of this book. Numerous large-scale development projects loosely labeled "new towns" are under way, and the potentialities have attracted some big corporations, including General Electric, Westinghouse, and Goodyear. Most of these developments, however, are not really new towns, much less new cities, but rather new suburbs or exurbs of old cities. Some of the projects, too far out to attract many commuters and lacking enough local jobs to thrive without commuters, face difficult and uncertain futures.

Amid all the present concern about congestion and pollution in metropolitan areas, the true new town, with its own economic base and its own cultural life, is an appealing concept. But for the next ten years at least, says an eminent housing expert, the new town is likely to be "little more than a cute toy for the Sunday supplements."

If land accounts for more and more of the selling prices of new houses, it follows inexorably that the houses themselves account for less and less. The purchaser, that is, gets less and less house for his money. And as a result of the generally high interest rates that have prevailed since the late fifties, the gap between purchase price and true cost to the buyer has run much wider in recent years than during the early fifties. The home-buyer finds, moreover, that he has to pay out more and more, and usually more than he expected, to keep up the house he gets. Rare is the suburban home-owner who has not been unpleasantly surprised by the high prices (and often poor quality) of home repair and maintenance services. And reliance on real-estate taxes to finance suburban schools and public services has imposed heavy burdens on owners of houses. Small wonder that houses become increasingly less attractive compared to garden apartments.

Since no important relief can be expected from rising land costs, burdensome real-estate taxes, or high-priced maintenance services, it is up to the home-building industry itself to try to provide more house for the money. Here it is possible to discern some flickers of promise.

Not very promising is the tired but still-invoked hope for big things from "new materials." New materials may help by reducing maintenance costs (plastic-coated siding, for example), but they cannot be expected to make much of a dent in the selling prices of new houses. More than three-fifths of the selling price of a new house represents land, on-site labor, the costs of putting in utilities, and the builder's financing and marketing costs, overhead, and profit. Building materials, new and old, with heating plant, lighting fixtures, and everything else including the kitchen sink, add up to somewhat less than two-fifths. The trouble with housing, indeed, is that materials account for too little of the total cost. What is needed to reverse the drift away from the one-family house is some reduction in the nonmaterial costs.

Wider use of prefabrication of housing components and of entire houses will gradually pare on-site labor costs. "We are going to see more and more factory-built components in housing, and less and less on-site labor," predicts Gene C. Brewer, president of U.S. Plywood-Champion Papers. Prefabrication shifts man-hours from highly paid hand labor, working under limiting craft-union rules, to less highly paid labor, working in factories with the aid of machines and industrial methods. That largely explains why mobile homes are so cheap compared to conventional one-family houses; the entire job, except for linking on utilities, is done in factories rather than at building sites.

Quite apart from the potentialities of prefabrication, there is a promising prospect of changes in the structure of the home-building industry. Twenty years ago an article in *Fortune* ("The Industry Capitalism Forgot," August 1947) noted that home building was "the one great sector of modern society that has remained largely unaffected by the industrial revolution." These words, regrettably, are still applicable to the industry. It was and is primarily an industry of small operators. About half of all one-family houses completed in 1966 were built by firms with a total volume of less than seventy-five units a year. Even the giants of home building are not very gigantic. Levitt & Sons, the biggest of all in dollar volume, put up 3,500 houses in 1966, about 0.4 percent of the total.

President William Levitt has voiced doubts that the home-building industry as presently constituted will be capable of building as many as two million housing units a year. "Management," he said, "is the single most important requisite in this business; it is our biggest asset. And management is what this industry does not have. It is not a very pretty picture. If there were 150 companies like ours—and there are none at the moment—I think we could build those houses. But as it is now, I can't see two million units a year any more than I can see myself jumping off the Brooklyn Bridge."

Fortunately for future buyers of houses, some big outsiders with well-known names and impressive credentials earned in other fields of enterprise have begun moving into home building. The most important short-run consequence of the interest in "new towns" is that it has attracted large industrial companies into housing construction. If they are not really creating new towns, they are at least getting into the housing business. Humble Oil has under way near Houston a new community planned on a Texan scale to house more than 150,000 residents. Other corporations that have moved into housing include Westinghouse in Florida; Boise Cascade, Occidental Petroleum, and Southern California Edison, all in California; McCulloch Oil and Goodyear in Arizona; U.S. Plywood-Champion Papers at Lake Tahoe; and Hallmark Cards in Kansas City.

The growing involvement of big corporations is the most encouraging new force in the housing field. Some of them are doubtless making mistakes of inexperience. But with their far larger financial and managerial resources, the corporate newcomers should in time prove much better able than small builders to hold down on financing costs, exercise quality control, schedule production efficiently, benefit from economies of scale, and market their wares effectively. The newcomers, in short, should be able to offer purchasers more house for their money. And by the force of competition, they may compel the housing industry to offer more house for the money.

Apart from whether the housing industry is capable of meeting the potential demand for two million units a year in the early seventies, many experts doubt whether enough mortgage money will be available to finance that many units —unless a lot of reforming is done in the meantime. With memories of the great mortgage crunch of 1966 still vivid in their minds, bankers, builders, and realtors are advocating reforms. They want changes that will both increase the basic flow of mortgage funds, and keep the flow from drying up when money gets tight again.

A diverse list of proposed reforms, some requiring government action and some not, emerged from a recent "mortgage round table," organized by Perry Prentice of Time Inc. Present were representatives of the National Association of Home Builders, the American Bankers Association, the Mortgage Bankers Association of America, the National Association of Real Estate Boards, the U.S. Savings and Loan League, the National Association of Mutual Savings Banks, the Life Insurance Association of America, building-products executives, mortgage specialists, and government officials. Some proposals from the panel's report were:

1. Wider adoption of the European practice of writing mortgages with variable interest rates. "The thrift institutions that put up most of the money for mortgages have to borrow on short-term the money they lend long-term. This may well be the number one reason for the feast-and-famine problem in mortgage finance. When money is tight, the thrift institutions find themselves stuck with a mortgage portfolio paying such low interest that the thrift institutions find it hard to bid in the open market for new money to lend." Under the variable-rate arrangement, the monthly payment remains the same, but the interest rate fluctuates as market rates go up or down (thus lengthening or shortening the term of the mortgage). In periods of tight money, accordingly, thrift institutions could afford to pay higher interest rates on deposits and so attract more funds. The report conceded that a shift to variable-rate mortgaging "would be much easier said than done."

2. More use of piggyback loans, "the most exciting new idea for tapping new sources of money for mortgages." A piggyback is a package loan combining a conventional mortgage and a smaller loan at a higher interest rate. It is a device for matching up what the borrower wants—a loan covering a very high percentage of the appraised value of the house—with what lenders are willing and able to provide.

3. Faster amortization. "The home builders could make their money problems much easier by switching their support to twenty-year financing instead of pressing for thirty-year

terms." The longer the mortgage life, of course, the smaller the monthly payment, but also the slower the build-up of equity. "Now that the dollar volume of trade-up sales to second-time buyers is more than twice as big as the dollar volume of new-house sales to first-time buyers, the builders have good reason to wish that faster amortization over the past ten years had enabled more of their trade-up prospects to build a bigger equity in their present homes to provide the down payments needed for the trade-up houses."

4. Simpler ways of borrowing on home equity. "Home mortgages are at once the biggest and clumsiest instrument of consumer credit in America. . . . We can see no earthly reason why a home-owner who wants to improve his home should need to pay for high-cost short-term consumer credit to finance it, just as if he had no security to offer. And if the mortgage has been paid down enough to create a substantial equity, we can see no earthly reason why the home-owner should have to refinance the whole mortgage if he needs to use that equity to finance his children's education, or a trip to Europe, or any sensible expenditure his equity brings within his means."

How big the housing boom will be in dollar volume, then, cannot be inferred from the projections of household formations. The potentialities spread across a spectrum. Construction of new units in the early seventies might amount to considerably less than two million units a year if the industry's capabilities are no greater than William Levitt has predicted, or if scarcity of mortgage money pinches housing starts. And the units built might include a very high proportion of apartments and lower-priced houses. At the other end of the spectrum, starts could run even better than two million a year, with a rich admixture of higher-priced houses. The difference between the two extremes, the worst-of-everything and the best-of-everything, amounts, on *Fortune*'s reckoning, to some $10 billion a year in the residential-construction component of GNP.

Just where along the spectrum the economic performance of housing falls will largely depend upon the housing industry: how many units it can build, and how much house it can provide for the money. More house for the money will mean more money for housing.

5

Home Goods: But What Will They Think of Next?

ANYONE WHO WONDERS whether the United States economy will be able to achieve full-employment growth over the next five years must ask where the demand is going to come from after Vietnam war expenditures top out. It's far from obvious that spending for cars and housing will be exuberant enough to take up the slack left by a slowdown in the growth of capital investment. Of the other consumer markets, one of the largest is home goods, the miscellany of durables that the Department of Commerce labels "furniture and household equipment." Sales of home goods account for 18 percent of total consumer spending on goods, excluding food.

From what can be seen at this moment, no vigorous spending thrust can realistically be expected in home goods either. Over the next five years, home-goods expenditures will probable increase about as fast as disposable income, i.e., about

4 percent a year apart from price changes. That would mean a rise in sales from $30 billion in 1966 to about $37 billion in 1971. It is hard to make a firm case for an appreciably better performance.

Home-goods sales were considerably stronger than that during the past five years, increasing a good deal faster than disposable income. They advanced $11 billion from 1961 through 1966, and in the process jacked up their share of disposable income from 5.3 percent to 6 percent. That percentage is higher than in many past years (see Fig. 13). Recent experience in appliances illustrates how hard it is to maintain a given share of expanding consumer income. Sales rose $2 billion from 1961 to 1966, but still barely kept pace with income. It was the same story with furniture in those years: boomy sales but not a significantly higher share of consumer income.

In view of the traditional importance of the home in the American style of life, it may seem surprising that home goods have had a difficult time maintaining relative market position. It may seem still more surprising that foreseeable trends in population and income cannot be expected to bring surging demand for home goods. When looking at the statistics, even the industry (if so diverse an array of businesses can be called an industry) sometimes gets carried away beyond the limits the figures really suggest.

For example, all branches of the home-goods business are very happily looking forward to added sales from the rise now under way in the number of new households formed each year. During the five years 1962-66, the total number of households increased by an average of 925,000 a year. During the five years 1967-71, the yearly increase will average, on current projections, about 1,182,000. The difference of 257,000 a year in net new households is certainly going to be a plus for home-goods sales. But the numbers have to be looked at in the context of a very big economy. When we remember that the total number of households in the United States is approaching 60 million, it becomes apparent that the extra 257,000-a-year complement of new families is not exactly going to swamp the home-goods market.

Looking at demographic projections in a somewhat different way, many home-goods producers see great promise in the prospect that younger families will be making up an

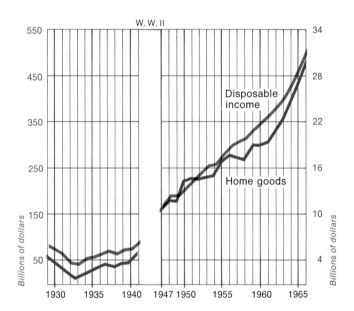

Home Goods Chasing Income:
A Long and Difficult Pursuit

Fig. 13. Sales of home goods have had a hard time keeping up with disposable income (chart at left). There were some great years after World War II when lots of new households were formed and consumers eagerly bought goods unavailable during the war. But later on income swept majestically ahead as home-goods sales paused or grew fitfully. Even the home-goods boom of recent years wasn't boomy enough to catch up with the income share of the early postwar years.

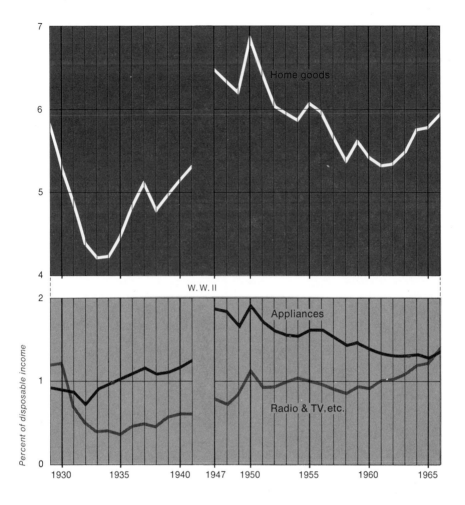

The relative meanderings of the two lines are brought out clearly on the upper section of the chart at right, which shows home-goods sales as a percentage of income. On the erratic record, it is impossible to say just what is normal here. The percentage was relatively high in 1929, fell sharply in the depression, reached a buoyant postwar peak in 1950, then went into a long downward drift until the early sixties. Despite the comeback, the percentage last year was not much higher than in 1929. The bottom section of the chart shows that the appliance and radio-TV percentages have moved almost inversely to each other. Appliances actually gained in the 1930s but subsequently tended to follow the general home-goods trend. Radios and other home-entertainment goods did much worse than appliances in the 1930s, but after the advent of TV this segment did much better than appliances.

increasing proportion of the total. Households with heads under thirty-five will increase from 24 percent of the total in 1966 to 27 percent in 1971. These households, as a group, spend more on many kinds of home goods than their share of the population would indicate. Last year households with heads aged twenty-five to thirty-four, 17 percent of total households, accounted for 23 percent of total home-goods expenditures. But again, the numbers are not all that impressive in the context of the entire economy. Households headed by persons thirty-five or older will still be accounting for about two-thirds of the market in 1971. According to Fabian Linden, consumer economics specialist at the National Industrial Conference Board, "The idea that the younger market is going to be the whopping market just doesn't hold up statistically." Younger consumers will be more important in terms of tastes and styles than in sheer dollar volume.

The prospect of a continuing rise in average family income also naturally figures in the industry's expectations, but the rise may not expand the home-goods claim on income. Higher income is of great importance for some products: families with pretax incomes of $10,000 or more account for 60 percent or better of the spending on bedroom suites, individual pieces for dining and living rooms, pianos and organs, wall-to-wall carpeting, china and earthenware, sterling silver and silver plate, clocks, pictures, and lamps. But on the whole, as a family's income goes up, its spending on home goods tends to *decline* as a percent of income. This is true of a family's total spending, of course, because as income rises, saving rises faster. But even as a percent of current *expenditures,* spending on home goods begins to drift down slightly somewhere near the $10,000 mark.

The industry is also placing a good many bets on selling consumers extra units of various products. No doubt there's a trend in this direction: families are buying a second set of dinnerware suitable for outdoors, a small additional TV set, a junior-size refrigerator for the patio, a portable phonograph, and—almost certainly—several radios. Last year there were 188 million radios in operation, or virtually one for every man, woman, and child. If 64 million auto radios are added in, the grand total comes to 1.25 per person.

This abundance of radios is inspiring product managers

for lots of other goods to dream big dreams. There are visions of nearly as many TV sets as radios in American homes. Some are speculating about small cooking units in recreation rooms or on terraces, and a miniature washer-dryer for every bedroom. One executive proclaims that it makes sense for all homes to contain at least two units of every small appliance. But very probably there are too many big dreams being dreamed at once. Some will come true, but not all, certainly not all at the same time, as trade talk sometimes seems to imply.

Whatever the proper discount on the industry's hopes, it is clear that a lot of the factors going for home goods in the past five years will not be present in the same way or to the same extent during the next five. One factor was that the general economic comeback from the 1960-61 recession brought a strong rise in consumer income. Impetus was later added by the income-tax cut of 1964, plus the subsequent reduction in excise taxes on appliances, radios, and TV sets. And all along consumers were energetically replacing their worn-out or obsolete equipment. General Electric estimates that in the years 1962 through 1966 replacement sales made up almost 60 percent of total major-appliance volume compared to 45 percent in the preceding five years. Replacement must have been particularly heavy in 1966, because home-goods sales advanced strongly in spite of the fact that housing starts declined by 300,000.

Another factor that has helped sales of home goods for a good many years has been price: the consumer has been getting more value for a dollar put into home goods than for a dollar put into many other things, especially services. Over the past several years furniture prices advanced less than consumer prices generally, and prices of appliances, radios, TV sets, records, and carpets actually declined (see Fig. 13), partly because of the production efficiencies that came from heavy investment in automation. Price trends will probably not be as favorable in the next five years. Carpet prices, particularly, are not likely to decline as much as before. GE, Whirlpool, and Gibson advanced their appliance prices about 3 percent in the spring of 1966, a sign of costs catching up with savings achieved through automation.

Even with all it had going for it, the home-goods market would have been appreciably less buoyant in recent years had not a spectacular new product, one that for some time had been standing in the wings, so to speak, taken center stage. That product, of course, was color TV. Color sales at retail bounded from a mere $90 million or so in 1961 to more than 4 million sets, worth something close to $2.5 billion, in 1966. Color TV thus accounted for just about all of the increased share of the home-entertainment side of the business (TV, radios, phonographs, records, musical instruments), from 1 percent of disposable income in 1961 to 1.45 percent in 1966, and for a sizable portion of the advance in home goods as a whole.

The home-goods market seems to require a genuinely new product every once in a while in order to keep pace with income. Over the decades, products of this character have included the sewing machine, the gas range, the phonograph, the vacuum cleaner, the refrigerator, the radio, and the automatic clothes washer. Some products, such as the electric iron, that represent a real advance are too low in price to have a big dollar effect. Others have a diffused impact because they catch on only gradually, in the manner of the dishwasher, the clothes dryer, and the air-conditioner. Still others occupy a relatively minor though solid niche, the floor polisher, for example, or carry on a sort of peripheral existence as giftware, a fate that may lie ahead for the electric slicing knife.

While completely new products are the more obvious supports of the industry, improvement of old products also helps to increase or sustain sales. The LP record gives new life to the phonograph. An elaboration of controls enables the washer to give a variety of treatments to a variety of fabrics. The refrigerator becomes frost-free. An authentic new style —modern—takes its place in furniture. Foam rubber appears for bedding, stainless steel for flatware, unbreakable plastic for dishes.

Lately the appliance industry has paid greater attention to making small appliances more convenient to use—more portable, more compact, and freed from entangling wires through use of batteries. Innovating on another front, the home-goods trades are moving more vigorously to cope with the repair problem. One solution is to offer the consumer a service contract at a fixed fee, a spreading practice. A newer one is for manufacturers to build appliances so that a worn

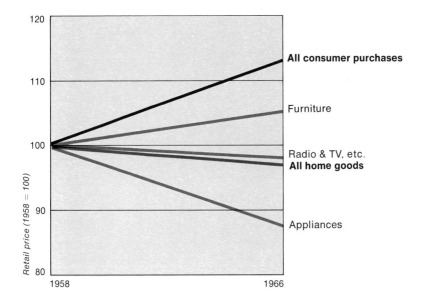

Fig. 14. Pleasant price behavior has helped sales. Retail prices of home goods are lower now than in 1958. Appliances, radios, TV sets, records, and carpets actually got cheaper over the years. And while prices of furniture and some lesser categories have gone up, they have gone up less than the index of all consumer purchases of goods and services.

or defective section can be simply removed and replaced. Proctor-Silex is on the market with a toaster, a steam iron, and a percolator of this kind, and Motorola with a color TV set. Increased mechanical reliability through use of solid-state controls is also in the cards. Of course, increased repairability or reliability does not necessarily expand an industry's sales. Indeed, it can help sales to have a product that is thrown away instead of being repaired. The transistor radio is an example. Something like 16 million radios, about half of total sales, were thrown away in 1966.

Sometimes old products begin enjoying a new wave of demand. In recent years, for example, many bare or skimpily covered floors have been carpeted. There has been a small-scale boom in the sale of musical instruments. Now coming up, some think, is a new interest in lighting—most American homes are poorly lighted from both a technical and a decorative point of view.

Still, the industry now and then needs a boost from a major new product. While color TV has played this role well during the last few years, it is already time to ask what will play it next. Color TV, to be sure, still has a long way to grow, but its most rapid gains almost certainly lie behind it. And there is nothing on the horizon that will take its place, not by 1971 at any rate. "Realistically," says an appliance executive who is understandably reluctant to be named, "I don't foresee any singular innovation which will be so readily accepted by the consumer that it will dramatically affect the market within five years."

The industry, of course, continues to work on important new products, but few have a prayer of making any large market inroads in the next five years. A home dry cleaner is one possibility. A microwave oven that can cook food very fast is on the market in a minor way. Somewhat more distant is ultrasonic cleaning for dishes—and perhaps even for clothes.

Some potentially big developments in consumer electronics lie ahead. Although a home video recorder can be bought now, it's for black and white only and the price of a thousand dollars or so takes it completely out of the mass consumer market. The addition of a special camera makes possible instant home movies, but that boosts the price another $300.

There is no certainty that a reliable color video recorder can be developed in the next few years to retail at a price that invites mass buying. Further away still is the home information or computer center, subject of some blue-sky talk.

There is always a possibility, of course, that some new product will become a blockbuster in the home-goods market within the next five years. But it would take quite a product to have as big an economic effect as color TV has been having. In a business pressing past $30 billion in retail sales, the impact of an innovation is bound to be somewhat muffled as a percent of the total market.

With the help of color TV, home-entertainment goods last year overtook both furniture and appliances to become the biggest home-goods line. Total sales came to approximately $7 billion, of which at least 40 percent was contributed by TV. This was not only a new high for TV, but also probably marked a turning point for it.

In 1966, sales of black-and-white sets declined for the first time since 1960, dropping by about a million, and sales continued to decline in 1967. In dollar volume, black and white is almost surely past its peak, if only because smaller sets constitute an increasing portion of sales; table and portable models made up 85 percent of the total in 1966. What the industry would like to see is a set with a weight of ten pounds or less, about a twelve-inch screen, and a price tag of around $50. Corning Glass and General Electric are separately trying to sell the idea of manufacturing a standard tube for all American set-makers so as to make it possible to produce such a set at a cost that could meet foreign competition. Last year 1,500,000 small sets were imported from Japan.

Sales hopes for 1971 come to about 5 million black-and-white sets, though Corning is talking 7.7 million. Unit sales of black-and-white sets can get that high only if prices are quite low, so the retail market would in any event not much exceed $400 million, less than half the 1966 figure.

The color-TV market also began to feel a change recently. Though unit sales about doubled to more than 4 million in 1966, there was a marked slowdown in the last quarter, and it carried over into the first half of 1967. So it begins to look as if the period of most rapid growth in color is over. Though industry forecasters agree that this is so, they differ about the precise shape of future growth. On some projections, retail sales reach 8 to 9 million sets in 1969 or even a bit more, and then level off or decline for a few years. On others, retail sales rise to 7 million in 1969 and keep advancing slowly to 8 million by 1971. Actual unit sales and dollar volume will depend upon, among other things, how much retail prices are reduced (in 1966 sets sold at an average of well over $500) and how fast the product mix shifts to smaller sets (consoles and radio-phonograph combinations accounted for 82 percent of unit sales in 1966).

On a down-the-middle estimate, the value of color sales five years hence would approach $4 billion, an increase of up to $1.5 billion. Since the value of black-and-white sales is sure to decline, the net gain for all TV is likely to be less than that. These calculations leave out the possibility that some astonishing product improvement, such as a technique providing a three-dimensional image, can be marketed soon at a reasonable price. But, says Bryce Durant, president of RCA Sales Corporation, there is little chance of anything like that in the next few years.

If the home-entertainment business as a whole is to hang onto its share of the market, it will have to gain a half billion apart from TV by 1971. It did a good deal better than that in 1961-66, and this suggests a kind of insurance in case TV revenues fall on the low side. One reason for optimism here is what is going on in the so-called audio market. Spurred by battery-operated portables and a young generation that loves the "big sound," more than 7 million phonographs were sold last year, making up about three-quarters of all audio-equipment sales. The share will be less in the future. Competition from tape recorders is mounting: at least 870,-000 were produced in the United States last year and 2,-800,000 were imported.

Newer and enjoying still faster sales growth is the cartridge tape player, which began life in autos and is now moving into homes. The user need only insert a compact cartridge housing a tape to get up to ninety minutes of sound reproduction or of recording time. The battle among the several varieties of cartridges and machines is reminiscent of the contest between various LP record speeds some twenty years ago. Cartridge players are not yet equal in sound quality to the older systems, and they turn hi-fi buffs off. (After all these years of hi-fi talk, there are only about 2 million hi-fi sets.) Despite the mounting sales of tapes and cartridges, sales of conventional records go on growing.

The radio business has been moving remarkable quantities of merchandise since the advent of the portable radio for personal use. Sales were stalled at around 8 million sets a year in the early 1950s, started to take off in 1956, and in 1966 reached the astonishing total of about 33 million— and that excludes about 9 million auto radios. Much of this gain is due to the availability of inexpensive imported transistor radios (radio imports came to 26 million sets last year), some of which can be bought for less than $5. But unit sales of radios have been running so strong that the dollar value of United States factory sales has been advancing even while imports have been pouring in.

Practically every consumer electronic product is in radio's position of facing import competition. In the last five years imports of such products have more than doubled, to about $300 million, and they are continuing to go up. While this is but 7 percent of the factory value of United States output, it represents a much larger percentage in terms of units. United States manufacturers increasingly respond by importing from abroad under their own brand names. Imports of radios under such arrangements rose to 4,600,000 sets in 1966 from 1,800,000 in 1965. RCA has arranged to procure all thirteen of its new tape-recorder models from Japan. To the extent, of course, that imports account for an increasing share of United States retail sales of consumer electronics, the market for domestic output of these goods will be narrowed.

General Electric calculates there are roughly a quarter-billion major appliances in the national household inventory, and that if every household were to acquire a full set of what GE calls the industry's "eight basic products," the inventory would nearly double. In other words, the appliance market as a whole is only about 50 percent "saturated." While a substantial majority of homes contain refrigerators, ranges, and clothes washers, the saturation level of air-conditioners, dishwashers, dryers, freezers, and food-waste disposers averages only about 20 percent. And only five out of ten important smaller appliances have achieved impressive saturation.

This may suggest that there is a great big market somewhere out there just waiting to be filled by an imaginative hard sell. But while the 50-percent mark can certainly be exceeded in the years to come, 100 percent will always remain beyond reach. The room air-conditioner, an undeniably useful product, has been around for quite a while and yet has achieved only 20-percent saturation nationally, and not quite double that in the hot Southwest. The public generally, it appears, continues to regard it as an optional convenience, not a necessity. And that is the position a lot of appliances appear to be in.

Still, saturation doesn't have to get anywhere near 100 percent to make a big market in appliances. In 1966 retail sales came to $6.8 billion. Sales of almost every appliance rose consistently from 1961 to 1966. According to data for a representative group of seven large appliances, obtained by the Daniel Starch survey organization, 16,530,000 units worth $3.8 billion at retail were purchased in 1966 compared to 10,770,000 units worth $2.7 billion in 1961. Sales of clothes dryers almost doubled, to 2,280,000. Dishwashers doubled, to 970,000. Some small appliances did splendidly too; sales of blenders quadrupled, to about 2 million.

The number of room air-conditioners placed in homes and apartments remained at about 1,400,000 units a year from 1957 through 1962, and then moved on to reach 2,700,000 in 1966. One influence, of course, is that Americans are getting accustomed to air-conditioning. Another is the rise in incomes—affluent people don't have to put up with hot weather. Still another is that units have become more compact, easier to install, and now raise fewer wiring difficulties, important attributes for a product that many people are apt to rush out and buy on the spur of a heat wave. And the smallest, simplest air-conditioner can now be bought for $100. Since these improvements won't be repeated again, sales are not expected to rise as fast in the next five years as in the past five.

Increasingly important in air-conditioning is the central residential system, which was placed into 238,000 homes in 1961 and into 653,000 in 1966. It's expensive, costing about

$1,100 in the average house (i.e., for a three-ton unit), and only 8 percent of the nation's homes have it as yet. The number in use may double in the next five years. People in the business predict that the central system will become an air "conditioner" in a fuller sense of the word—humidifiers and electronic air purifiers will be integrated into the system, with the average cost getting up to about $1,600.

Despite the increasing variety of products and the continuing efforts to improve them, the appliance industry's share of consumer income started to diminish once the burst of demand following World War II was over. In the past five years, however, it has managed to hold its share. To do so in the next five, it would have to raise its sales to consumers by $1.5 billion, half a billion less than in the past five. That much it should be able to do. A lively replacement market will help, for appliances have an average replacement cycle of about six years. Since sales of all kinds of appliances climbed from 1961 right through 1966, a large replacement market in the early 1970s is assured.

Furniture once accounted for more dollars than any other category of home goods but fell behind appliances after the war. During the past few years furniture has caught up again, and the two have been running neck and neck. For the next several years, the prospects look pretty good. Advancing levels of income and education are potentially more important for furniture than for, say, appliances.

Consumers have become more aware of style in furniture over the years. About a third of what is sold these days is Early American, and a slightly larger share is in various forms of contemporary; the rest is mostly in traditional styles of European ancestry, Mediterranean being the latest to achieve favor. Low, close-to-the-floor furniture, inspired by the informal habits of the younger generation, is gaining in popularity. With both skilled craftsmen and fine furniture woods becoming scarce and expensive, manufacturers are turning to new techniques and materials. The use of plastics makes it possible to turn out complex sculptured ornamentation at reasonable cost. In less expensive furniture, makers are using plastic to simulate a veneered look. Printing techniques can now imitate the grains of fine woods on inexpensive woods.

The Department of Commerce divides the remainder of

durable home goods into two groups. The smaller of these takes in china, glassware, tableware, and utensils (1966 sales: $2.8 billion). These products are likely to benefit more than other kinds of home goods from the growing number of marriages. Moreover, producers of these wares, which for many years underwent little change, have lately been innovating—nonstick pots and pans—and giving their products style and flair. Utensils have broken out of their old molds and now sport novel shapes and looks and vivid colors.

The remaining category (1966 sales: $6.7 billion) is a huge miscellany that includes carpets, pillows, blankets, lamps, mirrors, garden tools, typewriters, and so on. These "other durable house furnishings," as Commerce calls them, have increased their share of income in the past five years. In dollar volume, the big gainer was not a new product, but an old, old product, the carpet.

While there is no question that affluence and carpets go together, price reduction has contributed enormously to enlarging the market. In the past fifteen years or so, the average retail price per square yard sold has been nearly halved and yardage has jumped fivefold. Prices have come down for a number of reasons. The basic factor was the substitution of tufting for weaving; tufteds now account for 88 percent of all broadloom carpets. Tufting is done by a machine that punches fibers into a prepared backing, a method that has significantly lowered both capital and labor costs per yard. But even with the cost reductions resulting from tufting, carpet sales could not have expanded nearly as much without synthetic fibers; the supply of carpet wool is limited, its price fluctuates widely, and it has been more costly than synthetics. Prices of synthetic fibers have been trending downward for some time. Nylon now has 43 percent of the entire carpet market, and other synthetics 37 percent.

With synthetics, carpets are edging their way into hitherto unfamiliar places. Some varieties that are easy to maintain and clean are appearing in kitchens and bathrooms. The new specially treated polypropylenes and acrylics can be laid outdoors—on terraces, around swimming pools, and even on garden paths.

The carpet business has a rosy outlook for other reasons as well. Replacement is rising because carpets have come to be cheap enough so that people feel they can afford to buy a new one before the old one wears out. And large floor areas of the American home still lie bare, perhaps half of all dining rooms and master bedrooms. A new bullish factor is the recent decision to let carpeting be included in FHA mortgages; nobody knows how important this may become. Carpet sales have lately eased from the 15-percent average annual growth in yardage they have enjoyed over the past five years, but a healthy growth of perhaps 9 percent a year appears to lie ahead—more than double the probable advance of disposable income in constant prices.

When all the pieces are put together, it seems likely that home goods can maintain their 6-percent share of disposable income over the next five years. A great many uncertainties are involved here, of course. It's not certain, for example, that the years ahead will see enough innovation to keep the home-goods share of income from sagging. Moreover, demand for home goods is subject to a variety of influences that are hard to predict or even measure—shifts in styles of life and prevailing patterns of taste, and the resulting changes in how people decide to allocate their incomes. Consider, for example, the importance for the home-goods market of consumer choice between living in apartments and living in one-family houses.

Most of the new households will start out living in apartments, and there is some uncertainty about what they will do later on. A great many new apartment developments have sprung up in the suburbs, and this may mean that numerous families who in earlier days would have exchanged rented quarters in the city for houses of their own will opt instead for suburban apartment living as a way of life. If so, these families will probably spend less on home goods than if they were furnishing houses, if only because the space involved will be less. Unfortunately, no comprehensive study of the new apartment dwellers exists.

The home-goods market has a kind of special unpredictability about it. There is a very wide scope for optional consumer expenditures beyond basic utility, and there is no obvious limit to the upgrading process because it involves subjective values and feelings. "When you buy furniture, you buy appearance, environment, and atmosphere, not just sheer utility," observed Colin Carpi, president of General Interiors Corporation. In furnishing a home, the consumer confronts an exceedingly wide range of prices for products performing the same basic function: a table of a given size, say, can cost $50 or $500. Even at a given income level, families can make very diverse choices. It is impossible to say at what point a home is fully furnished and equipped—to furnish a home can take a lifetime.

While there is nothing so far to indicate a vigorous trend to accelerated upgrading, a potentially powerful combination of forces may someday make itself felt. The American is greatly preoccupied with his home, his aesthetic awareness is developing, and all the while rising affluence gives him an ever greater margin of discretionary income. Increasing affluence can be channeled in various directions outside the home—travel, recreation, apparel. But if the tides of taste and consumer choice run favorably, home goods may start absorbing a larger share of consumer income.

NOTE:

A serious effort to analyze the home-goods market soon encounters a haziness in the statistics. The industry's sales data extend no further than the factory or distributor levels, so precise knowledge of the units sold at retail and what they fetch is lacking. Some appliance manufacturers analyze the warranty cards their customers turn in. Others rely on sampling surveys, or base rough estimates on wholesale figures. One result of the lack of accurate retail data is that the total inventory position of individual products in retailers' hands is only sketchily known.

The total retail value of the consumer home-goods market, however, is known with a fair degree of accuracy. The Department of Commerce, making use of the Census of Manufacturers and other information, allocates the annual flow of production to consumers, to other users, and to inventory. Its figures for consumer expenditures understate the industry's *total* market somewhat. For one thing, appliances that are built into homes or apartments—central air-conditioners, central vacuum cleaners, exhaust fans, garbage-disposal units, and water heaters—are counted as outlays for construction. For another, the home-goods industry's sales of such things as unit air-conditioners and carpeting for business or professional use are allocated to investment. (Commerce hasn't yet had to decide how to handle the new practice of renting furniture, which presumably cuts into direct outlays by consumers.) For this article, *Fortune* has used Commerce estimates of consumer expenditures to measure the total market and its major categories. Figures for individual products come from a variety of industry sources.

6

The Great Fashion Explosion

"FASHION IS THE INGREDIENT THAT SELLS THINGS." That is how David Evins, a manufacturer and designer of high-style women's shoes, recently summed up his industry's extraordinary success in the last four years. Fashion has indeed been selling a lot recently: shoes and boots, colorful coats and vivid dresses, miniskirts and "fun furs," patterned stockings, pop jewelry, bows and belts; and men's colognes and tattersall slacks and turtleneck sweaters. As the list itself suggests, fashion has not only invested some familiar old products with a merchandisable new sex appeal, it has created mass markets for products that were quite non-existent, or quite esoteric, only a few years ago.

Thus it is now reasonable to talk about "fashion goods" as a large new market category. Traditionally, we have associated fashion with apparel, especially women's clothing and shoes, but that usage has clearly been overtaken by events. Today fashion is increasingly the something special in *all* clothing— including men's and children's and con sumers are expected to spend over $36 billion for it this year; their spending for footwear will run to an additional $6 billion. Furthermore, it is clear that fashion has made jewelry and watches ($3.5 billion) and toiletries and hairpieces ($5 billion) part of the same market. On this concept, fashion goods in 1967 accounted for more than $50 billion in consumer outlays, making this market second only to food among all consumer markets.

The market for apparel itself has been transformed in several different ways. For years apparel was a dullard, a laggard, growing less than consumers' disposable income in good years, and losing its market share over the long run. But in the last few years it has broken out of old patterns and has been grabbing a larger share of that income. And it is doing so without the benefit of any of the new technologies that spurred most growth industries, such as color TV. Consumer expenditures for apparel increased 40 percent in the period 1963–66—as much as they had in the preceding decade. Other consumer-goods spending went up by a third in the same four years.

Although the industry began to increase its share in 1964, it took a while to establish that the increase was significant. At first it appeared that apparel might have temporarily won some disproportionate benefits from the 1964 tax cut. But apparel held its relative gain in 1965 and jumped sharply in 1966; at that point it (including footwear) was getting 7.8 percent of disposable personal income, and jewelry and toiletries another 1.7 percent; in all, then, fashion goods had 9.5 percent, up from 9 percent in 1963. But even then most people in the industry thought it would slip back, and indeed sales slowed somewhat toward the end of 1966. Retailers, who had been raising their inventories and forward commitments to keep up with a sales boom that kept getting ahead of them, suddenly found themselves overstocked and overcommitted, and this led to an inventory recession in parts of the apparel industry during the first half of 1967. But that situation reversed itself, and sales and output rose again. Sales of apparel averaged 6 percent above the levels of the previous year. The 1967 figures made it clear that something pretty sensational was going on.

The fundamental change in the market may be viewed in relation to some other arresting figures. In the decade 1953-63, the 40-percent rise in apparel outlays took place while disposable personal income was going up 60 percent— i.e., spending for apparel grew about two-thirds as fast as income. If the same relationship had persisted since 1963, apparel spending would have risen 23 percent—not 40 percent. The difference between the two figures may involve sales of as much as $5 billion. The calculation is admittedly a rough one, but the magnitudes involved have been confirmed by a number of sophisticated econometric calculations; in any case, something like $5 billion may be viewed as the fashion industry's "bonus."

Down around Manhattan's Seventh Avenue and the other merchandising marts where fashion is a way of life—where "this season" and "that line" are the staples of conversation— they know that business has been good and offer several reasons for the gains. They talk about the number of women who are working; they talk about the impact of the swinging young generation; they talk about the sharp national gains in personal income.

As of mid-1967, 39 percent of women were working—a rise from 36 percent in 1963, from 33 percent in 1953, and 30 percent in 1947. Now there is no question that working women help the apparel market. The extra income of working wives certainly provides more money for clothes. Yet the fact is that during most of the period in which the proportion of working women was rising, the proportion of disposible income spent on apparel was declining. It is very doubtful that working women contributed much to the recent resurgence of apparel.

A more popular explanation of the resurgence refers to the special role of the numerous war and postwar babies, who are now in their late teens and early twenties—ages at which people are preoccupied with their appearance. This explanation of the fashion boom is oversimplified. True, the young do spend more on clothes—those in the sixteen-to-twenty-four age group spend 40 percent more than the average American, according to data from a special Bureau of Labor Statistics expenditures survey in 1960-61. And there certainly are a lot more people in this age bracket, about one-third more than were around in 1960. (Total population since then has increased only 9 percent.) But these swinging young spenders still constitute only 14 percent of the population, up from 12 percent in 1960; and meanwhile the number of elderly people, who spend *less* than average, has also been rising sharply. On balance, *Fortune* calculates, only 1 percent has been added to per-capita spending on clothing and shoes over the last seven years by changes in the age composition of the population. Age changes in the next three years may add another 1 percent. (It is worth noting, however, that population changes before 1960, when the fastest-growing groups were children and the elderly, were exerting a *downward* pressure on per-capita spending for apparel—4 percent between 1947 and 1960.)

When the industry talks about the importance of rising incomes, it speaks more profoundly than it knows. Discretionary income has grown mightily in the sixties, and there is a great deal of extra-extra spending money around. And the fashion industry has been offering the customers a lot to exercise their discretion on.

But the real point about that swinging sixteen-to-twenty-four group is not their spending power, but the fact that they have become market leaders. They have created a climate that has enabled fashion to catch on as a new force in the market, driving apparel expenditures higher and higher. Their larger share of the apparel market—they probably account for 20 percent of all expenditures now, compared to 17 percent in 1960—is greatly magnified by the fact that they are intensely interested in clothes; they are fashion prone, and they are able to communicate their love of fashion to others.

This avant-garde, thanks to that earlier baby boom, has now become a phalanx. And with all their busy fashion talk they have now enlisted in their ranks not only their older or younger sisters, but also mothers and aunts, who are no longer tied down at home caring for children. This is why fashion has become a new force in recent years—this and the fact that the young themselves have changed. Far more of today's girls go on to college and learn about a whole world of new ideas in art, taste, design, dress—living. Far more of them travel too, and so become exposed to still other influences on taste.

For a long time it has been a truism among sociologists

that Americans are especially inclined to accent youth and youthfulness; but that accent is now a drumbeat. "There is a big desire today to be young at all costs, to look modern, to look thin," sums up John Fairchild, who in seven years turned *Women's Wear Daily*, his family's staid trade paper, into the last newsy word in fashion, leading and epitomizing the whole change in the world of apparel. "In fashion there is no such thing as an old woman," says lawyer-turned-dress-manufacturer Jerry Silverman. (His partner, Shannon Rodgers, is a former architect.) "The whole look is young, from head to toe, because today we are *all* young."

The market consequence of the "youthquake" has been change, radical change, both in fashion and in dollar sales. Most of the change has swirled around women, who, according to the BLS survey mentioned earlier, spend over a fourth more than men do for purchased apparel (well over one-half more than men in the upper-income groups). Women spend additionally for yard goods, notions, etc., for home sewing. And if other "fashion goods"—jewelry, watches, colognes, lotions—are included, then women spend far more than men. The fact that women played the major role in making the fashion-goods explosion might, therefore, sound quite unsurprising. But women's spending for clothes, contrary to what one might suppose, has in the past been remarkably stable from year to year, rising and falling very little in the face of income changes. In their important study of *Consumer Demand in the United States, 1929-1970* (Harvard University Press, 1966), Professor H. S. Houthakker and Professor Lester D. Taylor have exhaustively correlated apparel spending with income and other influences. If things were on a normal course, their equations suggest, the recent income surge would have led women to increase their volume of clothing purchases only 15 percent per capita from 1963 to 1966; in fact, the increase was 22 percent. (These figures are corrected for price inflation; in raw dollars the difference was not 7 percent but 9 percent.) It is clear that only some vital new ingredient could have tilted the figures up so sharply. The ingredient was the great new fashion explosion.

William Barry, vice-president for J.C. Penney's soft lines, has explained how the industry has been doing a better job of competing for the consumer's dollar: "It used to rely more on meeting needs, but now it is really creating wants." "Yes,"

Americans Are Spending More on "Fashion Goods"

Fig. 15. Consumer outlays for "fashion goods"—clothing, footwear, jewelry, and toiletries—have risen by $15 billion, or 40 percent, in the past four years. The dollar rise equaled that of the prior fifteen years. Spending for apparel and related products increased its share of consumers' disposable income significantly for the first time in two decades. The long-term trend for this market has plainly been downward over the past forty years, but the drastic fall in the 1930s was interrupted and then reversed in the war and early postwar years. The reason was that consumers could not then get the cars, homes, and furnishings they were suddenly able to afford, and so spent heavily on apparel, even though absorbed by higher prices. Thereafter the fashion market's share dropped again, at first sharply, then more and more gently, until, finally, there was a new upturn in which fashion emerged as a potent new economic force.

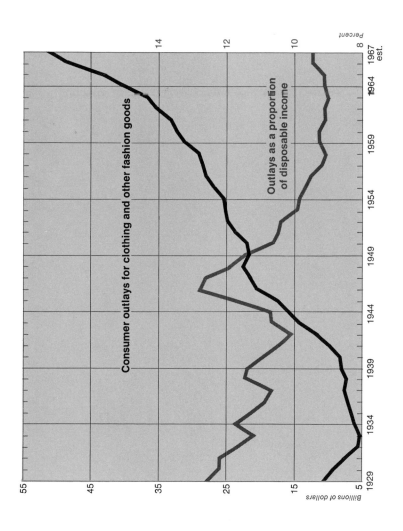

Consumer outlays for clothing and other fashion goods

Outlays as a proportion of disposable income

Percent

14

12

10

8

Billions of dollars

55

45

35

25

15

5

1929 1934 1939 1944 1949 1954 1959 1964 1967 est.

says Galen Hogenson, his merchandising manager for women's apparel. "Five years ago we relied heavily on basics. Now fashion change is the key to the whole thing." Selwyn Lemchen, vice-president of Interstate Department Stores, a leading discount chain, says that "the demand for new goods depends on the ability of the industry to create new styles, new colors, new fabrics."

New fibers and fabrics have played an underestimated role in creating some of the new demand. A. W. Zelomek, an economist who has been a consultant in the textile field for forty years, argues that the apparel industry has been helped considerably by the growth of synthetics—and that, contrary to a widespread impression, the growth has not come just at the expense of natural fibers. The new fibers shook up a lot of established promotional practices. The major synthetic producers adopted a strategy of promoting particular apparel lines while promoting their own fibers, and this forced the natural-fiber companies to revamp their own promotion. It is true, however, that the synthetics made possible real improvements in some kinds of apparel and in these cases were the biggest gainers in the expanded markets. Synthetics helped the growth of knits in all sportswear and, most spectacularly, in women's dresses. The new double-knit technique maintains the shape of dresses that formerly used to sag and bag. As double knits have become practical and economical, they have also become fashionable. Production has quadrupled since 1962.

Revolutions in fashion do not by themselves make revolutions in markets, obviously. When Christian Dior dropped hemlines almost to the ankle in 1947, everyone knew that something pretty revolutionary had happened to fashion. But the apparel *markets* do not seem to have been revolutionized. Women's outlays for clothing and accessories rose in 1947, but only because prices were rising; physical volume held steady. There was a further brief rise in 1948, but then outlays fell back, for several good reasons. Women were concerned with setting up homes and furnishing them with the durable goods that were finally pouring out of the factories. Apparel's share of disposable consumer income dropped steadily, right through the Korean War period; by 1953 it was down to 8.7 percent, from 10.9 percent in 1947. The 1953 apparel market, as *Fortune* described it at the time, was governed by the needs of a suburban housewife struggling to raise her children and make ends meet. What she wanted was a lot of simple, washable, inexpensive clothes—for herself, her children, and her husband. This period saw the beginning of the trend toward casual, informal wear. Women's "separates" became more and more popular, if not exactly "fashionable."

The world of fashion was next shaken up in 1957 with the introduction of the Balenciaga chemise. Widely known as "the sack," it created a brief flurry, only to lay a merchandising egg. Women were not yet ready to accept shapelessness, which was the fate of the style in the hands of both the mass manufacturer and the unskilled home sewer. Nevertheless, variants of the basic form persisted, for it possessed the virtues of ease and simplicity. The "little nothing" dress became a way of life for great numbers of American women. But uniformity presents problems of its own, and fashionable women began to resist it by using color. Support for the tentative move to color came from Jacqueline Kennedy in the early 1960s. She was, of course, a highly visible consumer of fashion, and many people in the apparel industry are convinced that she stimulated a good deal of popular interest in dress.

But dramatic change was yet to come. It is always difficult to generalize about the sources of great fashion happenings, but in the early 1960s, it seems pretty clear, the fashion winds that ordinarily blow across the Atlantic came from a new quarter. A group of young English designers, sparked by a bright young woman named Mary Quant, were making and selling something called the Chelsea Look to an eager young public. It was intensely "mod," a word that seems originally to have been just a contraction of "modern" but now has other overtones, some of them derived from the Chelsea Look itself: it involves bright colors, daring stripes, gay designs, limp forms, offbeat materials—and the short skirt.

Many people insist that by itself Mod could not have shaken up the fashion world. It seemed kooky, kiddish, a fad. Besides, it was pitched at the very young. Yet this time there was a new chemistry at work. In the mid-1960s fashion trends were being set not by an exclusive few but by a crowd. "There were so many young girls all around us," says June Weir, fashion editor of *Women's Wear Daily*. "They personified the spirit of the 1960s." The new Mod spirit even infected the Paris haute couture. This first became clear, not at one of the great traditional houses, like Balenciaga or Dior, but at that of a young newcomer, André Courrèges, who had actually been trained as an engineer. The Courrèges collection for autumn 1964 offered a new dress that was spare, cut straight, and short—short enough to need the small boots he also showed with it. And the colors were bright, or sometimes white. Courrèges thus put a Paris stamp of approval on the new international look and indeed brought to it new dimensions of taste and design.

Courrèges also confirmed a new relationship between designers and the crowd. "Designers aren't working in ivory towers any more," says June Weir. "They are watching and waiting to provide what the women want." Four or five years ago women often couldn't find what they wanted because—as the case was put by Herbert Levine, a daring high-style shoe designer and an early (1951) pioneer of the boot—"the IBM machine doesn't tell retailers what to buy the *first* time." The growing popularity of boutiques prodded the larger stores into getting with the new concept of fashion.

The new concept is rooted in a new life style. The young-in-heart new customers want to be able to move—clothes have become less "constructed," looser, shorter undergarments suppler, shoes more comfortable. They think of clothing not as status but as fun, and adventure, above all a highly individual matter. "All styles and colors and shapes have become available in the last two or three years," observes Elizabeth Hawes, for many years America's leading custom-clothes designer. "People *can* be more individual. There is no one look or style. Dressing can be a decorative art, and I think it will come to that."

To some extent it has already, Even only slightly snappy dressers are apt these days to find themselves buying clothes that in one way or another show a clear debt to modern art: in bold colors, in *fauve* and Mondrian-like prints, in the many op and pop effects. According to French furrier Jacques Kaplan, who helped revive a languishing trade by promoting "young furs" ("they're in the spirt of our time") instead of the "forever fur" ("an investment instead of a pleasure"): "The influence of people in the art world on fashion in the past four or five years has been tremendous." Artistic young

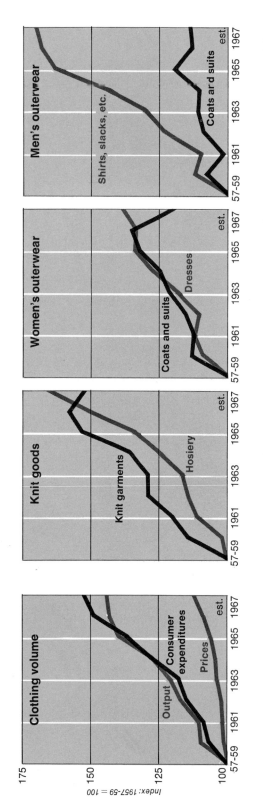

Index: 1957-59 = 100

Some Goods Are More Fashionable Than Others

Fig. 16. The fortunes of clothing producers have been varied. Doing very well are the producers of hosiery, of other knit goods, of a miscellany of women's clothing categories too small to chart individually (fur coats, for example) but important in the aggregate, and of men's shirts and slacks. The number of dresses produced has gained steadily, and consumers have upgraded their notions of how much they want to spend on dresses. There has also been considerable upgrading in coats and suits, for both men and women, but the unit trend there has been disappointing. Parts of the clothing industry have only recently begun to pull out of an inventory recession, which began early in 1967, when retailers found themselves overstocked after years of trying to keep up with soaring sales. Stocks have been worked down and output has been going up again now.

women searching for individual effects have taken increasingly to making their own "costumes," and Miss Hawes foresees, accordingly, a great revival in custom clothes and home sewing.

Most of the memorable fashion changes of the past half-century or so have had only limited or gradual effects on women's wardrobes. Designers have often come up with new and exaggerated concepts, but women have rarely accepted the whole argument—certainly not at first.

The latest round of fashion change—the "youthquake"—has been different, and *its* effects on wardrobes have been spectacular. The difference may be traced in large measure to the rather special consequences of those higher hemlines. True, hemlines had begun rising in a modest way in the late 1950s; but in the mid-1960s they moved several critical inches farther, culminating—presumably—in the miniskirt, which caught on explosively in early 1967. Even before that, several things had happened. One was that a lot of dresses that could earlier be shortened now ran into serious problems of proportion and cut. They could not go to the knee, let alone above it, with any kind of grace. Thus the shorter skirt dealt a real blow to a vast accumulation of clothes in women's wardrobes. The more rapid obsolescence of older clothes forced women to buy *some* new things. This pressure not only accounted for a sharp increase in unit sales, but also, since new styles tend to appear first in higher-priced clothing, it helped persuade a lot of women to pay more per unit.

The effects did not end there. Along with shorter skirts came another radical turn, a revolution of detail. It is the Total Look and involves the recent tendency of one thing to demand another. Once hemlines began to rise, other things had to change too. Women's legs were obviously in for a lot more attention, and women hastened to attend to them. Production of stockings rose steadily from 1963 to 1966, and has continued to rise. (In 1967, shipments in the traditionally weak first half were up about 20 percent.) And fancy stockings—brightly colored, patterned, glittery—are giving a lift to the market. Women may not wear them daily, but they want them at least for special occasions and special outfits, even at $5, $10, or $15 a pair. In addition, shorter skirts have accentuated what might be called the "peeping garter" problem, and have created a boomy new market for panty hose. Hanes Hosiery reported that, even after dou bling production of panty hose in the summer of 1967, it was still some two months behind in deliveries.

The short skirt also demanded a different shoe; the high-heeled, pointed-toe shoe didn't go with the new dresses either in proportion or in spirit. Accordingly, there arose a large new market for low-heeled, broad-toed shoes. These lent themselves to further artful invention: buckles, bows, balls, cutouts. They took well to color too, and looked smashing in patent leather, now a year-round favorite. Women were soon also sold on boots, which became fashionable in high, low, leather, plastic, and colored versions. Spending for women's footwear rose sharply in 1963-65. (Women account for well over half of total consumer outlays on footwear, and the total was up 11 percent in those years—and 12 percent more in 1966, to $6 billion.)

Other aspects of the Total Look have involved some impressive sales performances too. Jewelry has become much more important, and its variety is enormous; there are strong new markets for pop-arty plastic earrings, diminutive "antique" pins, and scores of other items. Sales of jewelry (including watches) increased by more than a third between 1963 and 1966, to nearly $3.5 billion. There are also expanded markets for undergarments. Girdles and brassieres have become much more comfortable in recent years; women readily accepted the introduction of Lycra and other spandex fibers, and now they are demanding, and getting, both color and color coordination. Even ophthalmic products—for example, those far-out frames for eyeglasses—have chalked up impressive gains. There is also a strong new emphasis on hair, for women have increasingly rejected hats and taken up hairdos and hairpieces instead. J. C. Penney, for instance, reports that better than a quarter of its "millinery" sales now consists of wigs, wiglets, and falls.

The Total Look doesn't stop there. For fashionable women, the list of "necessary" cosmetics has grown from a few basic items to a dazzling array that may well include eyeshadow, eyeliner, eyelashes, blushers, shaders, brushes. Within any such assortment, there may be further choices—special lipsticks, for instance, to go with special clothes. "It just takes a lot more thought to get dressed in the morning these days," says Frances Gardiner, a Neiman-Marcus market counselor.

A lot of businessmen with a stake in women's apparel are now wondering whether the recent heavy spending should be viewed as a "new norm"—or as just a single extraordinary splurge. Continued growth on the order of the last few years certainly cannot be taken for granted. Women's spending for apparel since the autumn of 1965 has at times had the quality of a great spree: in six months after that autumn, sales were up 14 percent. Sales leveled out after the first quarter of 1966; then, helped by the big success of the miniskirt, women's apparel spending turned up and rose in each quarter of 1967. But these gains left 1967 per-capita volume only about equal to that for 1966. The volume is still 5 percent above the hypothetical "norm" for women's apparel forecast in those Houthakker-Taylor analyses, which were prepared for the government's Interagency Growth Study. If the gains from now on were to adhere to the forecast rate, women's per-capita purchases would grow only about 10 percent in physical volume over the next five years. It is hard to believe that fashion will not help generate more growth than that.

Men's wear spending, up a third between 1963 and 1966, showed a further, rather surprising gain in retail sales in 1967. Like women's apparel spending, that for men is running about 5 percent over the levels forecast in the Houthakker-Taylor studies. Men's spending and women's spending do not usually rise and fall together. Men's expenditures ordinarily rise fairly sharply with income—and ordinarily sag fairly soon, as the men come to feel "stocked up." This time there have been anomalies, both in the amounts men have chosen to spend and in the things they have elected to buy. The greater part of their 1963-67 clothing spending was not for such "durable" items as coats and suits; here, in fact, may be, an untapped potential for further growth. (Military demand cut severely into civilian output in this area in the last half of 1966 and the first quarter of 1967, and stores had to run off stocks to meet sales demands.) Men bought, instead, a lot of informal clothing: trousers, shirts, sweaters, and playclothes. In this they simply continued the postwar pattern of casual dress, which saw the rise of "car coats" and jacket and slacks combinations for office wear.

A lot of men's spending has been spurred by technical progress. Permanent press, for example, outmoded a lot of men's clothes, even though it costs more. (One estimate is that permanent press adds a dollar to the price of a pair of pants.) According to one merchandising man: "It's a tough, tedious job to iron a pair of worker's pants. The wife was simply delighted to replace the wardrobe. In fact, she insisted on it." Permanent press, along with "wash 'n' wear," has also increased sales of shirts.

Several kinds of knit goods have added to men's wear sales, sometimes, it appears, with the help of fashion. When sales of plain knit shirts fell off, one chain put the accent on new textures, colors, and styles, with great success. "The men's area moves by evolution rather than revolution," says Cyril Johnson, Penney's merchandise manager for boys' and men's wear, "but even there things are happening. We used to be able to lay out a line of merchandise and live with it for six months. Now we have to look at it every month." Men have been experimenting for years, timidly at first but lately with increasing verve, with color and pattern in their sports wardrobes. And McGregor has actually promoted a "total look" for men—color coordination from head to toe—in its advertising for the fall of 1967.

Men's suits have remained pretty much the same for a long time, and most manufacturing and retail executives anticipate no revolutions. Bond Stores executives note a trend in the past two years to lighter-colored and patterned suits, but President Ellis Schechtman goes only so far as to say: "We're hopeful that this trend will continue."

The hopes are modest because of the sorry outcome of the one recent radical experiment in men's fashion—the 1966 rush to Mod in men's suits, coats, and other outerwear. "Mod moved in and out so fast that by the time we got the merchandise the time had passed," one of the brave innovators said. "It was too sudden, too extreme. We got carried away with it all."

But American men may yet get a heavier dose of fashion than they anticipate. At least one large manufacturer thinks the Mod misadventure was not an unmitigated disaster. He refers to it, only half in jest, as "research and development at the retail level," and adds: "Mod created a lot of interest in fashion. I think it advanced the timing. By the spring of

1968, every manufacturer will be showing something borrowed from Mod and such looks."

Furthermore, the standard American suit is being challenged by a string of name designers who made their reputations in women's fashions—John Weitz, Pierre Cardin, Bill Blass, and Hardy Amies. Genesco, a leading men's wear producer and retailer, has introduced a line of Amies clothing. The Amies suit silhouette differs from the ordinary run, featuring a longer coat, a nipped-in waist, and broader shoulders. Colors are soft blue, vicuña brown, and oyster white; for nattier spirits, Genesco offers plaid and striped variants. The Amies aficionado can buy, in all, some thirty items, all color-coordinated. In step with a rising nation-wide trend to "men's boutiques," the company has set up separate Hardy Amies shops in many of its Roger Kent stores.

Hart Schaffner & Marx has also detected some quickening of fashion interest among men. It is making many more models than it used to—suits with one, two, or three buttons, with side vents and center vents, double breasted and single breasted. "It used to be that most of the demand went to one style," says President John D. Gray. "Now there is an interest in three or four different looks." He expects that suit sales will accelerate in response to the greater variety of merchandise.

Are men, too, preoccupied by the fountain of youth? Some people in the business believe they are, and that their perking interest in fashion is being fed mainly by that preoccupation. But something more subtle may also be involved. The British fashion journalist John Taylor has speculated that men may simply be returning to the peacock ways that have characterized their dress through much of history. Says Taylor (in his book, *It's a Small, Medium, and Outsize World*): "The period where men have been sartorially reticent is but a fraction of the thousands of years of history which have seen them at least comparably colorful with women." Economist Perry Meyers, a marketing expert and consultant in the retail field, has offered the thought that men's clothing may be transformed by the new male-female relationships. "When a girl was going to be married and have two children, she wanted a man who looked like a bank clerk," Meyers observed. "She wanted a good provider. Now she has her own money. She has the pill. She is more playful. The men have to compete and attract attention to themselves." And this competition, he believes, may in time make a revolution in men's wear.

Any "fashion," of course, involves a sense of what is currently appropriate. But what is appropriate has traditionally been a question settled *for* the consumers. Today the consumers themselves make the governing decisions, and the new fashion expresses their own notions about beauty, taste, and humor. One result of this change is that fashion is a more potent market force than ever, whether it involves "fun furs" or op dress or elegant new colognes. The fashion industries competing for consumer dollars in this age of super-discretionary income have to run harder than ever. The race may well go to the nifty.

NOTE:

The apparel industry suffers from a plethora, not a dearth, of statistics. Many are not wholly reliable or comparable, owing to the diversity of merchandise made and sold, and to the large number of small (and changing) firms that make it. *Fortune* accordingly undertook to measure certain broad trends, and to corroborate some Commerce Department reports on apparel by use of several independent sets of data.

Sales data adjusted for price rises (plus or minus inventory changes) were checked against estimates of available supplies of goods. For example, Federal Reserve production indexes (based on many series for *unit* output) were adjusted in light of several benchmark censuses of manufactures; allowance has been made for increased values per output unit (over and above inflation) and also for rising net imports. Finding: apparel sales indeed boomed on the scale reported by Commerce. Statistical work for this analysis, and for the study of various factors affecting the demand for apparel, was performed by consultant Theodore E. Younger, under the direction of *Fortune*'s chief economist, Sanford S. Parker.

7

The Diverse
$10,000-and-Over
Masses

THE UNITED STATES was the first nation in which economic growth transformed the mass consumer market from a low-income to a middle-income market. This phase of economic evolution is now ending, and the United States is entering the era of the mass *high*-income market. By 1975, on *Fortune*'s projections, average family income after federal taxes will be around $10,000. Even today, 21 million families have incomes over $10,000, and they account for well over half of total income in the United States. This spread of affluence is transforming consumer markets and clearly has enormous implications for markets of the future.

Incomes cannot be expected to rise quite as rapidly in the period from 1967 to 1975 as they did during the period from 1959 to 1967. In this recent period, real disposable income rose about 43 percent. (Just since 1963, with the economy pushed along by a cyclical upturn and the effects of the Vietnam war, the advance came to 25 percent.) For the next eight years it is reasonable to expect that total real income will increase by more than a third. And with so many families now beyond the point where spending must go entirely for necessities, and able to exercise some discretion about what they buy, the stream of "discretionary income" will swell by considerably more than a third.

It is of course no secret that affluence is spreading in the United States. But data on the distribution of personal income after federal taxes—how many family units* receive how much of this income—have not been available since the Department of Commerce stopped publishing such data several years ago; its last figures are for 1962. *Fortune* undertook a considerable statistical effort to estimate the income distribution as of 1967 and, building on this and other information, to project the figures ahead to 1975. As was the case in the Commerce estimates, capital gains were not taken into account. It was assumed in making the projections that there would be no severe recession or large-scale war, and that national productivity would continue to gain at an average rate of about 3 percent a year. To eliminate the distorting effects of inflation, all of the income data were converted into constant dollars, based on 1967 purchasing power; the estimates and projections in this chapter are stated in these 1967 dollars.

One finding of the *Fortune* analysis is that the lower income brackets are shrinking noticeably, in general confirming the widespread impression that the number of persons living in "poverty" has been falling. The number of family units with incomes below $5,000 declined by something like 4 million from 1959 to 1967. Over the same span the number with incomes between $5,000 and $7,500 also declined, by about 3 million. The total of the two categories, 38 million family units in 1959, was down to 31 million in 1967. The number of under-$7,500 units will continue to decline in the next eight years, although at a somewhat

---

* "Family units" include families in the ordinary sense of the word, plus individuals living alone or with other, unrelated, persons. (People in institutions and some members of the armed forces are excluded.) It is roughly accurate to refer to all units with incomes of $10,000 or more as "families," since relatively few individuals not living with their own families have that much income.

slower rate. One reason for the slowdown is that the number of people in their middle, most productive years will show no growth at all, while the ranks of both young adults and of older people, who typically receive lower than average incomes, will be swelling. Another reason is that a residue of families headed by persons who are sick, uneducated, discriminated against, or otherwise handicapped will find it difficult to climb to $7,500 even by 1975.

Moving up the income scale, the $7,500-to-$10,000 group, 8 million family units in 1959, has grown to 9,700,000 and will grow about as much in the next eight years. Somewhat more family units are pushing their way up and into this class than are pushing up and out into a higher bracket. Within the bracket, life styles vary considerably. While an urban family of five living on $7,500 is apt to feel somewhat pinched, single individuals in this bracket are rather well-off—and there are about a million of them.

The big news about United States incomes is the extraordinary rise of those $10,000-and-over units. Their numbers are increasing much faster than the total number of family units. Eight years ago 17 percent of all family units had incomes of $10,000 or more after federal taxes. Today the figure is up to about 35 percent. In 1975 it will be approaching 50 percent—as these figures (rounded to the nearest million) make clear:

| | *Family Units (in millions)* | | |
	1959	1967	1975
Total	55	62	72
$10,000 and over	10	21	34

The bulk of the growth is occurring in the $10,000-to-$15,000 subgroup. Only 5 million families were in that bracket in 1959, but the number reached 14 million in 1967 and will be around 22 million in 1975. By that year there will actually be about as many families with $10,000 to $15,000 as with $5,000 to $10,000. Even the once-thin layer above, the families with more than $15,000, is coming to constitute quite a large market. The number of families above $15,000 has grown from 4,500,000 in 1959 to 7,500,000 in 1967; by 1975 it will swell to 12 million. Of these families, about 2 million will have from $20,000 to $25,000, and perhaps 1,500,000 will have more than $25,000.

In some ways the new consumer market is even richer than the foregoing statistics indicate. The $10,000-and-over families carry more weight than their numbers suggest. Their *average* income in 1967 was a hefty $15,000, three times the average for all other family units. When looked at in terms of the total dollars they command, *the $10,000-and-over families already dominate the American market.* In 1959 they accounted for 40 percent of all income. In 1967 they accounted for a bit over 60 percent. By 1975 their share should top 70 percent.

These rising percentages translate into enormous gains in buying power. In 1959 the $10,000-and-over classes had a total income of $150 billion or so. In 1967 it came to about $330 billion. In 1975 it will come to roughly $520 billion. The case may be viewed this way: in 1975, families with at least $10,000 will have more income—$145 billion more, in fact—than *all* families had in 1959.*

The massive growth of the $10,000-or-more income group has in part resulted from shifts in the occupational structure of the labor force, i.e., shifts into more skilled, higher-paying jobs (as opposed to the growth based on higher pay for the same jobs). However, effects of the occupational shifts have not been as great as one might suppose, given all the attention paid in recent years to the shift from blue-collar to white-collar jobs.

Those whom the government classifies as "professional, technical, and kindred workers" and as "managers, officials, and proprietors" together constitute little more than one-fifth of all employed persons, but people in such occupations head about two-fifths of all of the families with incomes of $10,000 or more. These proportions have stayed essentially unchanged during recent years even though the professional,

* The distribution of family personal income on which this chapter is based was prepared for *Fortune* by Paul Boschan, research director of the Guardian Life Insurance Company, who also worked out the figures for *Fortune*'s previous articles on the subject in 1954 and 1959. The 1959 article contained a forcast of income distribution for 1970, and present trends suggest that this forecast was essentially correct.

The estimates for this chapter would have put relatively more family units in the lower income categories if it had been possible to take account of *all* family units. Population experts think there may be about 5 million more people in the United States—mostly people with low incomes—than the Bureau of the Census was able to find in its 1960 count.

technical, and kindred group, the most highly paid of all, has grown at a faster rate than all others. The explanation is that the broad government categories contain many different kinds of jobs. It turns out, in fact, that of the nearly 10 million workers in the professional, technical, and kindred group, no more than half have incomes of $10,000 or more. While the ranks of such professionals as biologists, mathematicians, physicists, psychologists, and certain kinds of engineers are growing especially fast, the absolute numbers in these occupations remain small. Meanwhile, some very large "semiprofessional" groups, such as technicians who assist scientists, engineers, and the like, medical and dental technicians, and a whole variety of miscellaneous categories, are growing very rapidly too, and a good many of the people employed in these occupations earn less than $10,000 (many are women, many are young people). But increasing numbers of the semiprofessional jobs in offices, laboratories, colleges, medical institutions, research installations, and the like are going to be paying $10,000 or more in the years ahead as the demand for skilled back-up personnel continues to mount.

The semiprofessionals are beginning to make themselves felt as a distinct force in consumer markets. Many of the younger ones are educated enough, affluent enough, and confident enough of their futures to be among the consumption leaders of the day—those who eagerly adopt the latest fashions, buy sporty cars, take ski vacations in Europe. As time goes on, more and more marketing men will have to draw a bead on these semiprofessionals, or "white coveralls," as they have been called.

The semiprofessionals are in reality even more numerous than the government data indicate. Some people with a rather high degree of training are classified under nonprofessional categories—for example, even very sophisticated mechanics and repairmen, including some who service electronic equipment such as computers, are in the government's "craftsmen" category. The growth in computer-related employment seems to be in a class by itself. The Diebold Group has recently estimated that the number of computer operators and programmers is in the process of increasing from 122,000 in 1966 to 310,000 in 1970. Meanwhile, the top computer professionals—the systems analysts—will expand

IN 1975,
THOSE WITH INCOMES OF $10,000 OR MORE...

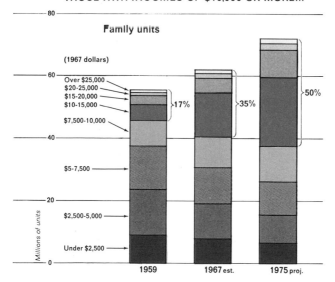

...WILL RECEIVE 70 PERCENT OF TOTAL INCOME

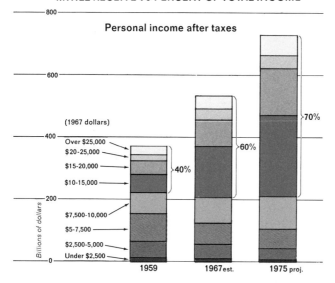

Fig. 17. Some 34 million family units will have incomes of $10,000 or more (after taxes) in 1975. Of these, 12 million will have incomes of $15,000 or more. The $10,000-and-over group will then constitute about 50 percent of all family units, as shown in the upper chart. The lower chart shows the shares of total income received by various income categories. The family units with incomes of $10,000 or more already account for 60 percent of total income.

from 35,000 to 160,000, a growth rate of 46 percent a year compounded.

The other major high-income category is that consisting of managers, officials, and proprietors. While the number of "managers and officials" has been mounting, many "proprietors" of small stores have been going out of business, and as a net result Fig. 18 shows only a small increase in the ranks of the total managerial group during 1959-67. The attrition of small businessmen cannot be expected to continue at past rates. Consequently, the category as a whole will show substantial growth in the future.

The $10,000-and-over group has been further swollen by gains in some groups not usually thought of as high-income. Median income for family heads who worked a full year as salespeople in 1966 was reported to be $9,572. (This figure is before taxes; the group includes, along with salesclerks who earned much less than that, many men who earned much more by selling complex manufactured goods, or securities, or insurance.) Many skilled workers in the construction and printing trades, over-the-road truckers, and craftsmen such as tool-and-die makers earn substantial incomes. And in automated and semi-automated factories, some employees who had jobs that were distinctly grubby twenty years ago and had to wash with Gre-Solvent after every shift have turned to watching dials and pushing buttons. They now wear a different garb—some of them, in fact, also wear white coveralls—and have higher incomes.

The fact of the matter is that the $10,000-and-over group is no longer middle class socially as well as economically; about three-fifths of all families now in it do not have professional or managerial status. The additional dollars that place many families in the high brackets are supplied by second or even third earners. Below $10,000, less than half of all families have extra earners. In the $10,000-to-$15,000 bracket, the number of families with extra earners jumps abruptly—there are nearly 8,500,000 such families, 60 percent of all those in the bracket. In the still more affluent income group over $15,000, approximately two-thirds of all families have more than one earner. Of the 21 million families who now have incomes of $10,000 or better, about 9,500,000 have a second earner; an additional 4 million have three or more earners.

More than 40 percent of the wives in high-income families work. This is a greater proportion by a good margin than in lower-income groups. One explanation of this paradox has to do with the age of the heads of these families: 60 percent have heads aged thirty-five to fifty-four. The children are out of their infancy and the wife is at least reasonably free to seek a job. Although a third of all women who work do so part time, and only 40 percent of the remainder work a full year, women nevertheless contribute perhaps a quarter of the total income of families with $10,000 or more. About 36 percent of all married women are in the labor force now, compared to 31 percent eight years ago. This percentage should grow over the next eight years, although probably at a slower rate.

About a fifth of $10,000-and-over families have more than two earners. This is also a much larger proportion than for lower income groups. Apart from young adults who are employed and live at home, about 9 million youngsters between the ages of sixteen and twenty-one work either part or full time and their numbers are increasing. Of course, this means that some families slip out of the $10,000 class after the children leave home.

The affluent families, then, have become a quite diverse group that includes a whole spectrum of occupations and encompasses rather wide differences in education and social class. What these families chiefly have in common is enough income to be able to exercise broad options in disposing of their income; and because they have so much of the total income, the options they exercise have great impact on consumer markets.

One of the basic options is whether to spend or to save, and it is a perennial question among economists whether rising affluence can be expected to lead to a rising over-all rate of saving. The question comes up because studies of how income groups allocate their money (the last comprehensive one was made by the Bureau of Labor Statistics for 1960-61) reveal that, at any point in time, higher-income groups save a larger fraction of their income than lower-income groups. The BLS data show that savings in families with incomes of $5,000 to $6,000 amounted to 1.3 percent of income, and that the proportion moved progressively up to 9.4 in the $10,000-to-$15,000 bracket, and beyond $15,000 to 23.5 percent. There is, then, a certain logic in supposing that as national affluence increases, the national savings rate will increase too.

But in fact the average level of income has been increasing for generations, while, as far as can be determined, the national savings rate has *not* risen over the long term. The paradox can be resolved by examining savings behavior at successive points in time. It is found that at any position on the income scale people tend to save at a lower rate than those with comparable incomes in earlier years. New products and new life styles keep standards of consumption advancing. In effect, the movement of people into the relatively high-savings brackets is offset by the tendency to save less in each bracket.

Still, the possibility of a long-term increase in the savings rate cannot be rejected out of hand: the future need not necessarily repeat the past. And whatever the future of the savings rate, the *motives* for saving will no doubt change, as indeed they have in the past. Very probably, relatively less will be put away for a rainy day or for anticipated major expenditures, and more of savings will be devoted to such matters as affording the husband a cushion to change jobs more often, or letting him take a sabbatical from work, or financing a safari for the whole family. The spread of such new motives for saving could conceivably be a factor that would raise the savings rate.

It is thus not foreordained that consumption standards will always rise as fast as income. That they can advance a good deal in a relatively short period of time, however, is attested by a recent study by the Bureau of Labor Statistics. It reports that an urban family of four, consisting of a non-working wife, two children aged eight and thirteen, and a husband aged thirty-eight, had to lay out $9,191 in 1966 for "what is necessary and desirable to meet the conventional and social as well as the physical needs." The amount is about 25 percent greater, in real terms, than a similar budget constructed for 1959; in other words, the standard of living is deemed to have gone up that much.

Just as it is difficult to project future savings patterns from data on the relation between savings and income in some past year, so it is difficult to project expenditures from such data. Nevertheless, it is instructive to look at some BLS

The Still-Expanding
White Collars

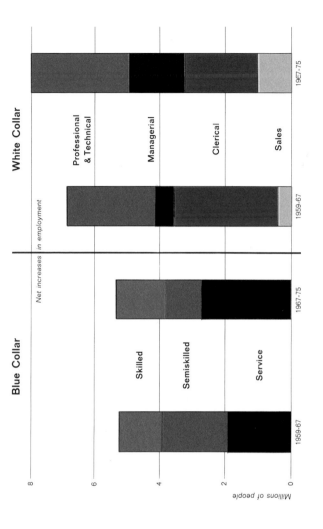

Fig. 18. This chart shows the net increases in various job categories (not the total numbers of people employed in those categories). White-collar jobs grew more rapidly than blue-collar jobs from 1959 to 1967, and the difference in growth has continued and will widen through 1975. The economy will add only about 5.3 million blue-collar jobs between 1967 and 1975, the same number as between 1959 and 1967. The number of unskilled workers (not indicated in the chart) will show no growth at all. The number of white-collar jobs will expand by about 8 million. There will be a slowdown in the growth of clerical jobs but distinct speed-ups in the growth of managerial and sales jobs. The "managerial" category includes proprietors, and its net growth has been held down in the past several years as many small proprietors have gone out of business.

figures for 1960-61 as a point of departure. In capsule, here is what they show. High-income families at that time devoted a perceptibly larger proportion of their expenditures than did lower-income families to alcoholic beverages, recreation, and education. Their outlays on clothing, eating out, and travel were particularly higher than average. The spending share for food eaten at home was less than in other groups; the share for buying of automobiles declined above the $15,000 mark. The high-income groups as a whole spent a relatively smaller than average share on housing, including utilities and all other matters connected with the house. But in the topmost group ($15,000 and over) the proportion spent for housing went up. This was mainly because the BLS housing figures included outlays for household help, outside laundering and cleaning, and repairs; in the high-income groups these outlays run relatively high.

With all the qualifications that have to be made in using such data for forecasting, it is still hard to imagine that certain particular markets won't benefit from plentiful income. Prime specific examples are Scotch, sterling silver, furs, pianos and organs, tickets to concerts and plays, private-school tuition, car rentals, and boating.

Efforts to project the effects of rising levels of affluence on patterns of consumer outlays are further complicated by differences between families with the same income. A notable kind of difference is that between white-collar and blue-collar families. The BLS data show that in 1960-61 blue-collars spent differently from professionals and managers of the same income level. Blue-collar families laid out more for tobacco and automobiles than the upper-status families, and less for cultural activities and housing. Lower expenditures on housing—including home furnishings—have been explained by Social Research Inc., headed by Dr. Burleigh B. Gardner, as resulting from the propensity of working-class wives to seek mostly "comfort" while middle-class wives are more interested in appearance, "something that conveys a visual impression that corresponds to some more or less explicit standard of taste."

Patterns of consumer behavior associated with social status are slow to change, and their extent and durability can easily be underestimated. Some years back, for example, it was widely believed that in moving beyond the city line many millions of people were adopting the same set of suburban manners, morals, and spending habits. Later research suggests that this just isn't so, that suburbia does not "homogenize" its inhabitants. There are diverse suburbs, and if a particular suburb seems homogeneous, that is probably because it is inhabited by people who were socially and economically alike to begin with.

Nevertheless, there is *some* tendency toward convergence in consumer habits, in cities and suburbs too. For example, blue-collar people eat out more often than they used to, and they increasingly buy the same kinds of apparel as white-collar people. And for all kinds of families, a move to suburbia does involve certain appurtenances—at least one car, outdoor play equipment for children, the paraphernalia of lawn care.

While there is some tendency for class differences in consumer behavior to wane, powerful forces are making for greater diversity in consumer choices. Every day, it seems, American consumers have a greater variety to select from. New products and designs as well as novelties and fads come along in swift procession. This plentitude itself encourages people to express their individuality as consumers, move beyond yesterday's boundaries, and buy things they haven't bought before.

Affluence enlarges the area of individual choice—a fact that is recognized by the label "discretionary" as applied to family income beyond some specified level. The pool of discretionary income, already very large, is spreading wider and growing deeper. If all income above $7,500 after taxes in each family unit is considered discretionary, then, at present, discretionary income, shared by 31 million families, totals $180 billion. By 1975 discretionary income will be in the hands of about 46 million families, and the total will come to roughly $280 billion.

As this enormous pool of discretionary income continues to expand, consumer markets will increasingly depend upon choice, fashion, fad, even whim, rather than need. With the passage of time, consequently, advertising and marketing men will be paying more attention to competition between diverse categories of goods and services, even between alternative styles of life. More and more consumers will have enough income to make large discretionary purchases—

choices among such alternatives as, say, a vacation home, a trip abroad, a swimming pool, a boat, a second or third car. One particularly momentous kind of consumer choice is whether to live in an apartment or a house. A fundamental choice of this kind brings a train of spending consequences. A man who buys a house takes upon himself a long series of expenditures for a great variety of goods and services, including everything from pruning shears and patio furniture to the services of roofers and plumbers.

And, increasingly, in purchases large and small, it is the proliferation of kinds and styles of goods that moves the dollars. This proliferation has for some time been conspicuously evident on supermarket shelves. In apparel, "The Great Fashion Explosion" has brought new arrays of shapes, colors, and textures to widen the range of consumer choice. In autos, the abundance of nameplates, variations, and optional extras is such that the possible combinations run into millions. By exercising available options, a purchaser now can buy a mass-produced car that is unique, different from any other on the road.

Another kind of choice that affluence can make possible is choice between more income and more leisure. One of the beckoning rewards of money has traditionally been leisure in which to enjoy it. For the working class, there has been a long-term trend toward shorter work weeks and, more recently, a trend toward more paid leisure too—longer vacations, even sabbaticals (for example, for steelworkers with high seniority).

Herman Kahn and Anthony J. Wiener of the Hudson Institute, in their recent book, *The Year 2000*, contemplate the possibility of a "leisure-oriented" work pattern, with a seven-and-a-half-hour day, a four-day week, thirteen weeks a year off, and ten legal holidays. The total number of work hours a year for a full-time worker would come to 1,100, not quite 60 percent as many as now.

On a straight-line trend, the Kahn-Wiener scenario implies that by 1975 the work year would be reduced by something like 200 hours—roughly four hours a week, equivalent to more than a month of additional vacation. It seems unlikely that a decline that large will come about over so short a span of years. Agriculture aside, the work week hasn't been reduced that much in the past generation. The really significant reductions have occurred as a result of major social decisions: the cut from twelve hours a day to ten in the nineteenth century, the advent of the eight-hour day and the five-day week in the first third of this century.

But even if overwhelming amounts of leisure are not likely for a while yet, the average work year will doubtless shrink somewhat. For example, as additional income becomes more marginal, workers will seek less overtime and moonlighting income. Movement in that direction is already visible in statistics on moonlighting: the number of people holding down two or more jobs, about 3,600,000, is no greater now than it was ten years ago.

Whether or not people trade off much income for leisure, it is virtually certain that a larger and larger share of total consumer income will go for leisure or leisure-related expenditures—sporting goods, camping equipment, travel, and admissions to games, shows, and cultural events. A great many families, it can be expected, will be acquiring second homes for weekend or vacation use.

Along with greater income, and a greater variety of consumer choice, the coming of the $10,000 average family income will be accompanied by some heightening tensions. The widening disparity between the incomes of the prosperous masses and the poor will bring increased pressures for measures to shift a larger share of total income toward the bottom of the scale. (The share of income received by the lowest fifth of all family units has not improved since the days of the New Deal.) As things are going, the feeling of deprivation is bound to mount. The average annual income of family units with $5,000 or less after taxes is now about 31 percent of the average income of all family units; this ratio will decline to approximately 27 percent in 1975. Since these figures do not take account of capital gains, they somewhat understate the actual disparities.

The prosperous masses will also be encountering a different sort of tension, for which it is hard to imagine any effective remedy. As more and more people become affluent, demand for some things comes greatly to exceed supply, and these are often things the supply of which cannot easily be expanded. The effect of so many dollars chasing a limited supply is evident in the dizzying inflation of prices for certain kinds of nonreproducible goods, such as works of art and antiques. More widespread in its effect is the growing imbalance between the supply of and the demand for certain services. The list of services already in short supply includes household help, resort reservations during the peak season, space in marinas, and tickets to various attractions, including plays, professional football games, the Metropolitan Opera.

The rising standards of society tend to reduce the supply of some services. The number of people willing to do housework or yard work, for example, diminishes even as demand for these services increases. "I've finally become rich enough," a Ford Motor Company executive observed not long ago, "that I can afford to pay somebody else to cut my grass. But now I can't find anybody willing to cut it." It is a kind of lament often heard in the land.

The state of affluence, then, seems less rewarding to some as more and more people become affluent. Increasingly, people find that greater income does not readily purchase some of the amenities they would like. This fact of life may come to have important economic consequences. It is conceivable that, because they can't get what they want, consumers sometimes won't spend as much as they might.

This consideration bears on a broad question raised in the first chapter: whether aggregate demand will be sufficient over the next several years to sustain full-employment growth of the economy. Though blurred at present by the special effects of Vietnam-war requirements on the economy, this remains a pertinent question for the future. The adequacy of demand will to some extent depend on how desirable consumers find the goods and services available to them to purchase. At any rate, businessmen involved in supplying consumer goods and services can look forward to a very big stream of income to fish in.

Index